COPYRIGHT

Copyright © 2014 by Tiffani Neilson Creations, LLC.

All rights reserved. No part of this publication may be reproduced, distributed, or transmitted in any form or by any means, including photocopying, recording, or other electronic or mechanical methods, without the prior written permission of the publisher, except in the case of brief quotations embodied in critical reviews and certain other noncommercial uses permitted by copyright law. For permission requests, write to the publisher, addressed "Attention: Permissions Coordinator," at the address below.

Tiffani Neilson Creations LLC
8275 S. Eastern Ave Suite 200
Las Vegas, NV 89123

Author: Tiffani Neilson
Cover Photo: Tedd Bliss
Copy Editor: Martin Coffee
Web Developer: Justin Inabinett
Graphic Design: Tiffani Neilson

Photography by: Charles Too of FotoManiacs, Laurent Velazquez, Lauri Kaye, Dana Sol, Mikey McNulty, Hew Burney, Beau McGavin, Jeremy Womack, William Jaye, Tedd Bliss, David Heasley, The Rock Bear, Marcel (MLive9), Thomas Stark & Jeff Ragazzo.

Copyright (c) 2014 Tiffani Neilson Creations, LLC. All rights reserved.

ISBN: 978-0-9915282-1-9

HOLON PUBLISHING

Published by Holon: www.Holon.co
Creative Community for Authors, Artists, Businesses and Non-profits.

TABLE OF CONTENTS

Copyright	ii
About the Author	v
Dedication	vi
Disclaimer	ix
Foreword	x
Chapter 1 Welcome to Fabulous Las Vegas, NV!	1
Chapter 2 Understanding Your Purpose	6
Chpater 3 21 Things you just do not do in Vegas	11
Chapter 4 Arriving in Vegas	18
Where to Stay	20
Chapter 5 Adapting to Your Surraoundings	23
Chpater 6 Entertainment & Dining	30
Chapter 7 Off the Strip	39
Golf	43
Chapter 8 Better Safe than Sorry	44
Chapter 9 Think of the Savings	51
Shop till you drop	53
Outlet Shopping	53
High-end Shopping	54
Shopping Malls	54
10 Ways to Save	55
Chapter 10 Girls vs. Boys	57
Bachelorettes	59
What to Wear	61
Top Spas in Las Vegas	62
Going out with the Boys	65
Chapter 11 VIP Clubbing	68
Nightclub List	74
Nightclubs off the Strip	77
Chapter 12 Tools for the Pools	79
Chapter 13 After Hour Power	83
Where to find After Hours	86
Adult Entertainment	86

Chapter 14 Tricks are not just for Kids	88
Magic Shows	90
Local Street Magicians	90
Magic Stores	91
Fortune Tellers	91
Chapter 15 Local Life	93
Chapter 16 Checking Out	99
Chapter 17 Plus Tip	103
Chapter 18 702 Trivia	107
Facts for Foreign Visitors	108
History	108
Haunted Vegas	109
Vegas Now	110
Chapter 19 FAQ	112
Chapter 20 Are You a Survivor?	117
Chapter 21 Glossary	122

SECTION 1

ABOUT THE AUTHOR

Tiffani Neilson is the author of the much-anticipated book, the Sin City Survival Guide. Originally from Ohio, this small town girl gives her perspective on how to survive in Las Vegas.

Crowned "Vegas Prom Princess 2010," Tiffani Neilson has been leaving her mark on Sin City for the past 5 years. Tiffani was honored as a Distinguished Woman of Nevada for her work as an entrepreneur. She has been in commercials, public service announcements, voice-overs, and featured as a guest on Vegas TV & Fox 5. Tiffani's press releases have been featured in more than 100 news outlets around the world.

Tiffani Neilson is currently Creator/CEO of PetBlaster Inc. PetBlaster.com is an online website described as, "Your One Source for Everything Pets.™" She also works as a freelance web developer, graphic designer & artist Tiffani is listed as one of the Top 10 Graphic Designers in Las Vegas.

With a background as an entertainment artist, Tiffani hosted a series of events at the Cathouse in Las Vegas, known as the "Neon Nights in Sin City Experience." Her past work as a go-go dancer at Eve nightclub and as a promoter/host for multiple venues makes her the perfect person to write a book about what to expect from Las Vegas.

Friends and fans in Columbus, OH remember Tiffani for her contributions to the community and for her impact on their local nightlife, through her clothing design & event company, Klever X.

Tiffani Neilson has always had a passion for motivational speaking and feels this book echoes what every tourist & local should know about the infamous Sin City.

DEDICATION

This book is dedicated to LAS VEGAS & all the people that love this incredible city! I love Sin City & want to enlighten both those who have or have not visited Las Vegas.

I dedicate this book to my family (especially my Mom, Dad, Brother and Grandma- AKA Nana), friends, fans & my pet-Kitty McFlipperson.

A big shout out to George! He was there when I got the brilliant idea. Thank you for being such an inspiration in my life. Miss you. ;)

My Sin City Survival Sisters featured in the book:

Meka, Neldy, Kim, Danielle, Nicole and Ivana.

Thank you to my sponsors: RawFusion, FotoManiacs, Accelerate Solutions and 24:7 Limousine. Thanks for adding a grand entrance to my elaborate outings.

My AMAZING photographers!!!

Thank you to Rick Lofton, Meka Coxon, Neldy Cabulong and Justin Inabinett, for your continued enthusiasm for success.

Bill & Stacy this sock is for you. LOL.

My friends from home that make me so proud of my efforts to elevate nightlife in Ohio, and now around the world.

The teachers that have encouraged and educated me throughout my life, especially Jon Sun, Mike Seiler, Mrs. Halterman, Mrs. Mahaffey, Mrs. Carpenter & Mrs. Call.

All the Vegas VIP hosts, promoters, security & bathroom attendants that have hooked me up and shown me the ropes. You guys rock!

Tao Group, Light Group, Angel Management, Thirty Three Group, Next Events, Las Vegas Weekley, SpyOn Vegas, Seven Magazine, Xpense Group, Choice Party Life and all the LV promotion/media teams.

Paul Chosy for making me move here.

Lyndsey Merriman for the one-way ticket that changed my life.

Josh and Deborah from 702 Inc.

Rich DiPilla from Vegas TV.

Jim Nico & Dr. Jane Karwoski, the Social Network Show.

Howard from Circle Builder.

Bridget Hockert for my Vegas 101 education, priceless.

Bethany Gonzales, Steve Aaronoff, Owen, Neil, Cuban Dany, Adolfo, Glenn Dekoven, Ida Masotto, Chauntel, Cassandra, Breeana Dominguez, Donald Glaude, Jeff Davis, Jennifer Corson, Jeremy JBFF & Cailin>Landon Cash$, Donnie, Brittany Starr, JR, Drew, Kevin Forte, Mikey Spikey, Chris Fun Son, Bobbi Jo Quick, Amit & Bobbi, Clarence McGee, Sklyer Haze, Lisa Brandt, Lisa Marie, William Campbell, Serafina, Ryan Kessler, Dan Yillianes, Billy Scott, BoTown, Tonya Hayes, Hugh Wesley Robinson II, Bilge, Sonny Nguyen, Rick Jones, Aric Nelson (Cage), Nicole Sergio, Cory McCants, Willie Clemente, Donna, Sylvia Bradley, Brandy Hope, Angie Alcantar, Gooby, Tarah Lee, Joey, Rita Gomez, Trouble, Casey, Jeremy Gotwals, Joe P Miami & Patricia>Baby Benjamin$, Brit Bliss, Julie Fox, Joy, Kevin Coxon, Cameron, Leona, Joe, Damien Patton, Georgette Dante, Ray Poe, Al Wagner, The Loftons, Damian Hidef, Jet Dones, Bradley, Kumar, Jennifer Moelter, Mondo, Angela Dracula, Chella, Jenny Keifer, Epyk Crew, Mr. Fun, Dr. Scott, Jenn, Sandy, Gee Jeed, Leo, Freddy Figz, Andrea Deleon, Kim Phillips, Thom Svast, Stellar, Gino Lopinto, Joey Mazzola, Scottyboy, Mike Attack, Adam, Steven Greene, Chad Noyes, Jeff Glass, Damien Jay, Tiffany Masters, Cindi & Justin, Joe Meltdown, Sean Kurker, JJ Flores, Partyrock, Chico, Brian Shae, Theresa Ryan, Matrix, Alvin Diehl, Jasmine, Syrus, Drazpa, Chad Vegas Vibe, Thor, David Poulsen, Anastasia, Clyde, Matt, Tiffany Anderson, Katie Reese, Yessica, Andrew & Jessica, Zoe, Sarah Jane Woodall, Ashley USC, Ted, Jazmin, VIP Travis D, Simon, Bella, Ernie, Dora, Ferzan, Heather Smith, Mikey, Beau & Dave, Paul Jost, Jenna Gold, Faamous Ericc, Terrance, Aaron, Malia, LA, Angelina Kissa, Leo, Leora, Leon, Ledina, Lea Luna, Lisa & Dom, TJ, Stephanie, Tralisha, Bilge, Angela Makeever, Blades, Zachary Sin Vegas, Haley, Taylor, KO, Katie Badley, Pammy, Nino Anthony, Chris Garcia, Kris Nillson, Miguel, Dino, Nathaniel Dei, Mike Haas, Kat, Tammy, Brian Campbell, Zack Taylor, Emil, Derek Anthony, Greg Matta, Aseem, Billy, Allen Montalvo, Andre, Linda, Matrix, Erica Moore, Megan, Kina, Bella, Sarah Sheller, Carissa, Justin Key, Ashley, Cassidy, Scotty Twist, John Musso, Marshall, Johnny Diesel, Oscar, Alex, Dennis, Mike Attack, Dougie Fresh, Sherry, Shon, Everett,

Jaqueline, Rebecca Horsh, Kerry Simon, Michelle, Mina Kahn, Johnny Savage, Soto, Brad Spieser, Brandon Walker, Rebecca Richards, Michael Nelson, Chris Fields, Danny Roma, Mike, Whitney, Rick Landers, Brian, John & Bibi, Dana, Vinny Cane, Neal Conlon, Johnny Vegas, Nora, RJ, Allen Ladd, Dave Evans, Brian Pfeiffer, Jay Farber, Jordan Stevens, Lisa & Katie Pikus, Stacy, Cameron Shadow, Billy Wickes, Crystal Cox, Shay (Unique Styles), Angela, Keaton, Dragon XL, Vincent Do, Barbara, Garveys, Aton, Nico, Jackie, Jacqueline Potter, Dragon R, Fly, Kelly, Darryl Awesome Owens, Stacia Higgins, Jaimi Haidan, Turron, Bobby, Joel Pizzels, Ali G, Danny Chasen, Ben Farrell, Ryan, John K, Alicia Cary, Jo Smith, Tabitha, Denaro, Garcia, Charles Armstrong, Jamie, Jason, Jay Campanile, Syrus, Paul, Monkey, Deamon, Donny, Frank Charles, Crimm, Renatta, Darko, Sean Sappington, Paul, Dr. Alan, Terje, Robert, Wyman, Dan Sherbondy, Rob, Ace, Neldy's Mom, Ivana's Mom, Tess, Shadow, Dez, Sunshine, Funktrain, Janessa McElroy & family, Sadaf, Sarah, Sean, Seth, Sky, Erica, Toya, Victoria, Natassa, Nate, Nicole, Margo, Gene Ford, John Picard, Tom Starker, Pam Theodotou, BoMA Bob, Mike G, Jillian, Deborah & Bryan, Katie Badley, Cameron Peppers, Natalia, Snyder, Randy Haffey, Petey, Phil, Vic, Mojo, Sammy, Carissa & Brandon, Fat Lip Tattoo, Rob Wolford, Anthony Atalla, Benny Benassi, Andy Dick, Tom Green, Pauly Shore, Snoop Lion, Joel AKA Deadmau5, Jenny McCarthy, Coolio, Jojo, Lizard, Tommy the Greek & Dominic.

RIP Tiffany Doran, Bert Bonner, L & Woody Lewis.

Thank you to ALL of my amazing friends that helped me to understand what life is really about. If I did not mention your name, it does not mean that you are not important or special to me. I am just saving the full list for another book that focuses more on all the unbelievable people that I have been fortunate enough to experience life with. Thank you for all the lessons and memories.

DISCLAIMER

THE VIEWS REPRESENTED IN THIS BOOK ARE THE IDEAS AND OPINIONS OF TIFFANI NEILSON.

ALTHOUGH I AM A VERY THOROUGH FACT CHECKER AND A CLOSET TECH NERD, THE FACTS & STATISTICS

IN THE BOOK ARE AS ACCURATE AS POSSIBLE.

THIS DISCLAIMER IS SIMPLY A REMINDER THAT THE STATEMENTS AND ASSUMPTIONS YOU ARE ABOUT TO READ MAY NOT BE CURRENT BY THE TIME YOU READ THIS BOOK.

THINGS IN LAS VEGAS CHANGE ALL THE TIME. PLEASE SEE THE WEBSITE FOR UPDATES AND ADDITIONAL INFORMATION AT WWW.SINCITYSURVIVALGUIDE.COM.

BE SURE TO DO YOUR HOMEWORK & GET PLENTY OF REST BEFORE TESTING YOURSELF TO SEE IF YOU HAVE WHAT IT TAKES TO SURVIVE IN SIN CITY.

FOREWORD

"Life comes at you fast, but Vegas comes at you nonstop."

I am sure you have heard the phrase "Only in Vegas." The question is, where does this never-ending domino effect of chaos end?

My craziest Vegas experience would have to be in August 2009, when I was offered a gig go-go dancing in the Real World Suite at the Palms, for a Beacher's Madhouse, TV pi-

lot.

I did not know what to expect, but it definitely was not what awaited behind the door...which was 4 Oompa Loompas, 3 Easter Bunnies, 2 Transformers (that actually lit up), Batman, Superman, Captain Jack (& both pirates from Treasure Island,) the little Monkey that does tricks on Las Vegas Blvd (LVB), and many other interesting characters.

This was by far the most abstract and creative guest list I had ever witnessed, as I still wonder...

How was I chosen to be a part of such a motley crew?
Things that make you go hmmmm......

Las Vegas is a city where you could win big or lose it all quicker than you could ever comprehend. Life out west is definitely action packed, putting your values, health and wealth to the test.

I live each day by leaving the past in the past, the future in the future, and being in the moment. Knowing your purpose and maintaining your focus is the only way to achieve success in Las Vegas.

Going with the flow and trusting my instincts were enough for me to get by when I first decided to move to Vegas. However, before I knew it I was floating so freely, I had no idea which direction I was heading anymore.

I feel at some point everyone comes to a crossroad where you begin to question life. Who am I? What is my life purpose? Where am I supposed to be? Why am I here? When will I find my purpose? How will I figure it all out?

Well, you don't have to have it all figured out to move forward. All anyone essentially needs is a little direction.

One day I was reflecting on life with my good friend George and we were discussing how so many people in Las Vegas are so lost. Not just the tourists, but the locals as well. Spiritually, physically and mentally; these people visiting and living in Las Vegas need some divine guidance.

It was at that moment that a light bulb turned on in my world. A single idea, and the actions I took to make this book a reality, ignited a creative explosion. Once I chose what purpose I was going to serve, the faster things began falling into place.

Originally from a small town, I have always felt the need for adventure. While living in Columbus, Ohio, I fabricated my career as an Entertainment Artist (Klever X).

Not only was I featured on NBC4, but I also take pride that I am remembered for holding some of the most fun & creative events to rock the Midwest. Everything is better in a costume...well al-most everything.

Leaving my family behind, I took my chances and drove across the country with only what would fit in my Honda Accord.

There are plenty of TV shows that give you a glimpse at how socially complex the Strip can be. Yet that does not even begin to highlight the emotional and mental strength required to endure the absurd expectations it takes to qualify as someone that is VIP in Vegas.

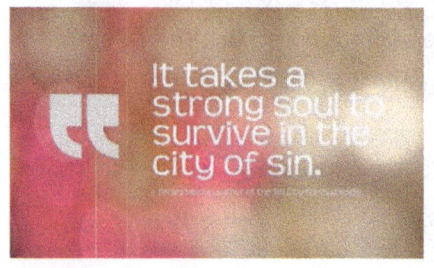

My first 3 years here I went out every day, every night, everywhere, for all things VIP. If there were 8 days in a week, I was out 10. There is always something unbelievable happening, but if you are a local, there are so many perks that it is hard to resist the constant stream of once-in-a-lifetime invites.

Once you are welcomed into the "industry" scene of the local 702 nightlife circuits, you soon realize there is always a party going on somewhere.

Eventually, I came to the conclusion that I could only ride the wave of never-ending activities for so long. At that point I moved to the edge of town and got a pet. Now that I have moved beyond my "newbie" or "rookie" stage, I tend to lock myself away at my laser bachelorette pad as much as possible to write this book and develop www.PetBlaster.com. It takes serious discipline to refuse invitations to party with celebrities at some of the most sought after venues on the planet.

It may sound outrageous, but Las Vegas truly does feel like home. I was never on my high school homecoming court, yet by a landslide victory in 2010 I was crowned "Vegas Prom Princess." Botown Productions' annual Vegas Prom has been voted " Industry Party of the Year." It is quite different from a high school prom, but a popularity contest nonetheless.

The path that I have chosen has not been easy but it has been fun. In fact, living in Las Vegas has elevated my soul to its highest highs and humbled me to my lowest of lows.

When it comes down to it, I love my life and consider Las Vegas a paradise of opportunity and would not want to be anywhere else. I can honestly say I could not be happier living the exciting life of a Las Vegas Local. I have always been categorized as a "party girl." With 24-7 entertainment by the world's most talented people, this is definitely the city I belong in.

For those of you that live here or have previously visited Las Vegas, I hope this book renews your love for this incredible city. Unfortunately I have had to witness many people grow jaded from spending years living this exhausting lifestyle.

For any of you reading that have not had the opportunity to visit Sin City, what are you waiting for? Seize the day! Carpe Diem! Live in the moment! Start packing and plan your next trip.

1

WELCOME TO FABULOUS LAS VEGAS, NV

Also known as: the 702, Sin City, Lost Wages, Entertainment Capital of the World, Gambling Capital of the World, Marriage Capital, Breakup Capital, Capital of Second Chances, Glitter Gulch, The Strip, City of Light, Social Network Capital and yes the city is even known as the Silicon Strip (for all of you tech lovers out there).

My personal favorite nickname for Vegas and probably the underlying reason why I chose to live here is; "The Biggest Little City in the World."

LIGHTS, CAMERA, ACTION!

Sunshine, 24-7 entertainment, 5 star dining, gambling, celebrities, world renowned nightclubs, excitement, magic and action await you in Las Vegas.

Almost everyone around the world has visiting Las Vegas on their bucket list, but it takes a rare breed of people to actually want to live here. Without a goal, a plan and strategy your chances of survival are slim.

In this city of nonstop entertainment and limitless options available to you at all times, I have found that the most crucial part of enjoying Vegas is knowing where to go and when to go. Who you know is another vital piece of this puzzling city. Holidays, weather, and the convention calendar are also factors that play a significant role in how all business is handled day to day.

If there is one thing that you can count on in Vegas, it is change. Las Vegas is constantly evolving in entertainment, architecture and technology. Innovative ideas are welcomed and placed into our lives daily.

Las Vegas Boulevard is one of the most iconic and recognized streets in the entire world. The 2.2-mile stretch of this legendary street has had several name changes in its history, such as Fifth Street, Arrowhead Hwy, Los Angeles Highway, Salt Lake Hwy, US 91, US 93, US 466 and State Route 6.

Staying current on the local hot spots, new venues and fashion frenzies is a full-time job for industry locals. The Sin City Socialites, or in Vegas "localites," set standards around the world for what's hot & what's not. Those that are aware of their surroundings can reap the rewards of making the most of the opportunities that are available.

"If you can make it in this city, you can make it anywhere." -Lauri Kaye

ATTENTION PLEASE

When in the city of Las Vegas, it is very important to pay attention. Attention to what? Everything. Obviously you want to avoid any type of dangerous situation, a pickpocket thief, broken glass, mysterious contents being slipped into your drink, etc.

Consequently you also should have a general idea of your location. Knowing where you, your car and your friends & family are can be very useful information. Even though plans can change in a moment's notice, it is important to have an idea of where to find the people with whom you are traveling.

Keep your eyes open for celebrities, giveaways, or you may even find some cash on the ground.

WHERE?

When in directional doubt, just know the Stratosphere is on the North side of the Strip towards downtown/Old Vegas. The downtown area is in a slightly different part of town that is past the Stratosphere. This is where the Fremont Street Experience and many government offices are located.

The center of what is considered the main drag of the Strip is found at Flamingo and Las Vegas Boulevard, near the new ferris wheel called the High Roller that will be complete in 2014. Another secret is to use the light coming from the Luxor as a nighttime navigation system. The giant beam of light bursting from a pyramid is your Sin City compass, it points to the Southeast.

"What happens in Vegas stays in Vegas?" Right? Wrong. The things that happen in the Entertainment Mecca of the Universe grasp the attention of headlines around the globe and even those in other galaxies.

Las Vegas is one of the most fascinating, fun, and accepting cities in the United States. Sin City opens its arms to diverse cultures, activities, beliefs and lifestyles. With a constant flow of tourists coming to visit and an eclectic group of residents, which consider Las Vegas home, the dynamics of these mixed lifestyles is extremely interesting. It is almost as if everyone in the city functions with a vacation mentality, in which smiling is highly encouraged. With near perfect weather year-round and a constant party everywhere you look, a smile should be effortless.

Sin City Survival Guide™
Las Vegas, Nevada

The main strip of Las Vegas is 2.2 miles of glittering lights and endless entertainment.

Be sure to check out the new Ferris Wheel, the High Roller located at the Linq, opens in Summer 2014.

Old Vegas found just North of the main drag of the strip and is becoming more tech friendly through businesses like Zappos and the Vegas Tech Fund. This is also where the Fremont Street Experience and many government offices are located.

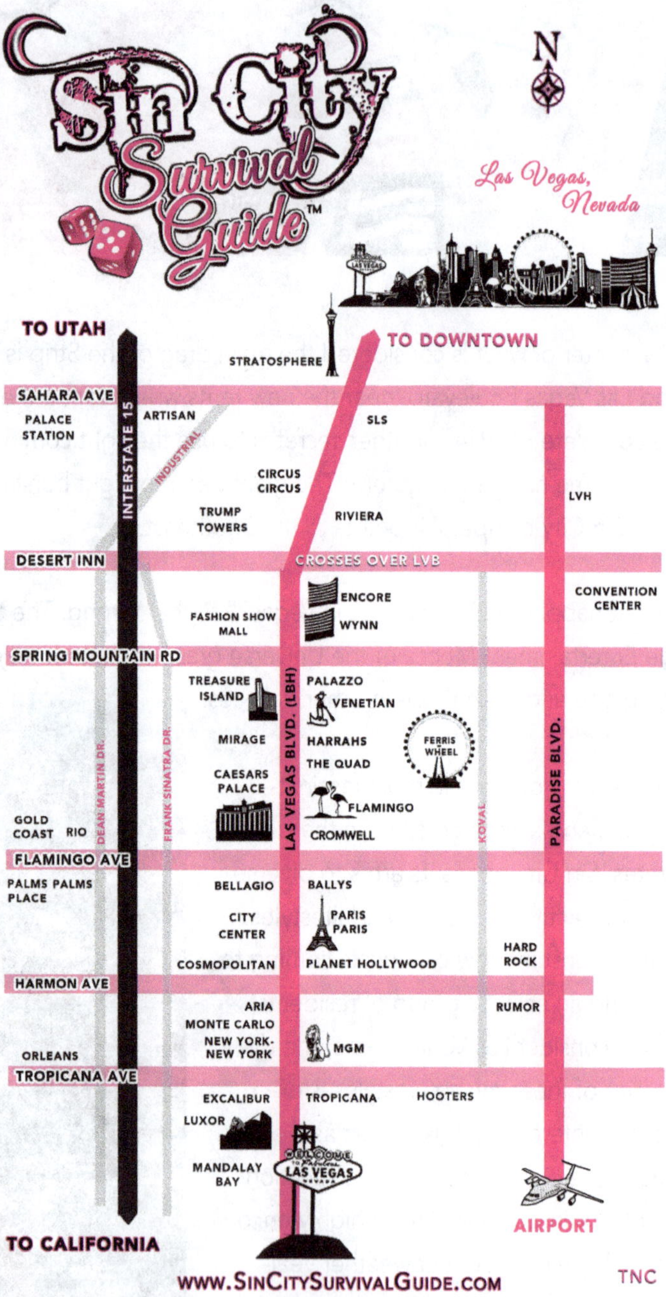

www.SinCitySurvivalGuide.com

TNC

2

UNDERSTANDING YOUR PURPOSE

Once you have decided on what you want from this city, the easier and quicker you will enjoy yourself to make the most of your time here.

For one reason or another this book has gotten your attention. More than likely, this is because either you live in Las Vegas, have visited or are planning to visit Sin City.

A little structure can go a long way. The key to success is deciding upon what you are trying to accomplish with your time... yes even in Vegas.

Perhaps your purpose is business related, in which case there are multiple trade shows and conventions happening weekly covering almost every industry in existence.

Many visitors arrive with the goal of partying till they drop. This is probably not the best idea. With a mindset like this, chances are you won't even remember most of your vacation or life... that is if you survive.

With even a minimal amount of planning and a goal or two, you can still party & get wasted without wasting your time.

If you are considering starting your life over or relocating, Las Vegas is a great choice, due to the number of networking opportunities and weekly rentals are available at affordable rates.

This is definitely a city that makes almost anything a possibility (that is if you have the right resources). Suddenly, things that once seemed impossible are readily available in the Entertainment Capital of the Universe.

Celebrities are within a mile from you, just about anywhere on the strip due to the increase in filming movies and TV shows (not to mention the shows & photo shoots). Your opportunity to be a superstar is available at auditions every day if you just look for them.

This may sound shocking and although it is rare, I have heard people say they do not like Las Vegas. My feelings are that those individuals had no idea what they wanted from the experience and became stuck with the leftovers of people who knew what they wanted and how to get it.

I do not understand how anyone could ever be bored here. Vegas is constantly in the spotlight, bringing visitors from around the world to partake in the city's extreme culture. People have a general "vacation" attitude year round, making Sin City the perfect destination for any season.

There is just something about this fabulous city that captures the attention of billions of people. Outlaws, celebrities, performers, gamblers, dreamers and visitors have been drawn to this valley of excitement & adventure since the Wild West was established.

Life in the desert is unpredictable; you are coerced to live in the moment.

When I reflect back on my purpose, I see that my direction has changed course several times, yet kept its focus. I love Ohio and thought I would never move this far from home, but I could not ignore my magnetic attraction to Sin City.

Since the journey moving across the country, Las Vegas continues to deliver year after year, with unlimited opportunities.

Currently I am CEO of PetBlaster Inc., and feel I am right where I am supposed to be. As a child, I never saw myself as living in Vegas running a social network for pets and writing a book on how to survive in Sin City, but it just goes to show that anything is possible.

Living in Las Vegas will challenge your mind, body and soul. It is one thing to take a trip to Las Vegas, however it is an entirely different ball game when you live here.

My best friend Meka is the creator of Raw Fusion Foods, which promotes healthy living by offering recipes, spice kits and more. Her tagline is "Saving the world starts with you.™" As a natural born leader, she lives every day for her purpose.

Life is a gamble...and Luck is preparation meets opportunity.

I have always been a big fan of lists, so my suggestion is to make a list of all the things you would like to see and do. I have already started a bucket list for
you but feel free to add any places, shows, dinners, clubs, etc. The sky is the limit. Choose your destiny!

VEGAS BUCKET LIST

1. Ride the roller coaster at New York-New York.
2. Be one of the first to experience the new Ferris Wheel.
3. Zip line down Fremont Street.
4. Go out to one of the biggest nightclubs in the country.
5. Attend a "DayLife" pool party.
6. Go up inside the Stratosphere and experience the thrill rides.
7. Test your luck at gambling.
8. Go to a strip club, the Rhino is the most legendary in the city.
9. Ride in a limo or drive an exotic car.
10. Snap a pic at the Welcome to Las Vegas sign.
11. Walk the Strip.
12. Shop at one of our world-class shops and boutiques.
13. Go hiking at Red Rock.
14. See the Hoover Dam.
15. Go on a helicopter tour of the Strip.
16. Watch a Cirque du Soleil.
17. Go on the gondola ride at Venetian.
18. Have a late night breakfast of steak and eggs.
19. See the fountains at Bellagio.
20. Go to an after hours party.
21. Eat at one of the Vegas buffets.

3

21 THINGS YOU JUST DO NOT DO IN VEGAS

1. Don't trust everyone.

Trust no one! My dad has drilled this point into my head from early childhood and I am forever grateful, as it has saved me from many dangerous situations. Although I tend to focus on the best in people and things, I still recognize the negative aspects. Being aware and being afraid are 2 entirely different things.

2. Don't forget your ID.

In Las Vegas you need your ID all the time. It does not matter who you think you are or how old you think you look. You will be carded more here than you could even imagine.

3. Don't expect too much.

Expect the unexpected. In all my experience, I have found that setting high expectations leads to disappointment. If you expect nothing at all, you find far greater satisfaction with your results.

4. Don't believe everything you hear.

The more someone is bragging about who they are and what they have, it is typically because they are trying to be someone they are not. This is a city which makes it very convenient for people to live a "fake life."

Do your homework. It is always best to double check if someone tells you there is free entry at an event or show times, etc. Everyone has played the game telephone, things can easily become distorted.

5. Don't get caught up!

With anything available upon proper request, too much of anything can turn from a blessing to a curse...Quick! From gambling to food to drinks to sex to excitement to many other options. The truth is too much of anything can lead to destruction, addiction or worse.

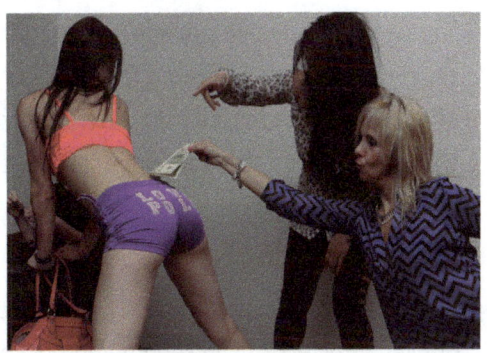

6. Don't drink the tap water.

Very simply, this is just not a good idea. That is unless you have absolutely no other option. In desperate measures, some form of H2O is better than none at all.

7. Don't take your shoes off.

No matter how bad your feet hurt, being shoeless can lead to even more torture. You should not take off the heels and walk the Strip as if it is sand on the beach... The casino floor, parking lot and Las Vegas Boulevard could easily damage your feet by filth, sharp objects, or many other unexpected obstacles.

Remember: shoeless= clueless.
Wear shoes that you won't be complaining about, or ignore the torment. They always say beauty is pain and shoes are an essential part of fashion. "If the shoe doesn't fit, bring flip flops."

8. Don't assume the cab driver is going to take you the quickest, most cost-effective route.

Just as you will come across several people that will give you accurate information and charge you a fare price for your requests, there are others that do not have your best interests in mind. Some taxi drivers have been known to take the "long route" or the path of more traffic, in order to increase the cab fair. Simply ask your driver in a polite manner if they can drive the most direct route to your destination.

9. Don't jaywalk.

Besides the fact that you could be ran over, you also face the risk of getting a ticket or even arrested. I have seen numerous reports on the news of pedestrians losing their lives and heard stories of people being fined large sums of money.

10. Don't let bad luck continue.

If you're having a bad luck kind of night, don't just continue to gamble. Just get some sleep or do some sight seeing to give yourself a chance to attract some better energy, rather than spend your savings at the same slot machine waiting on the big payout. Set yourself a spending limit to ensure you have enough cash to last your entire trip.

11. Don't set your purse or wallet down!

Your best bet is to bring only the items you definitely need with you. These valuable items should be kept close to you at all times. Just because your friend is at the table doesn't mean she is going to keep her full attention on babysitting your belongings. Las Vegas has many distractions, so just keep your things on you and save yourself the trouble of having them disappear.

12. Don't use your phone while gambling!

It does not matter what casino you are in, the rule remains the same. When playing card games at a table, you cannot use your phone. You have to walk away from the gaming tables to make calls or text.

13. Don't count your chickens before they hatch.

If you are counting on receiving anything, wait until it's actually in your hands before considering it yours or part of your spending money. Sometimes things will not go as planned or things will occur to change your expected results, no matter how solid you may think your plan is.

14. Don't lose it.

Losing even your claim ticket will end up causing you a huge headache. This advice should also be applied for your room key, especially if your name does not happen to be listed at the front desk for your room. Other items you may need to take extra caution in avoiding losing would be your phone, ID and especially your clothing. I have heard horror stories of lost shoes and other missing articles of clothing that could easily lead to awkward stares from onlookers.

15. Don't drink anything and everything.

You do not want to leave your drink out of your sight or accept drinks you did not see being poured for you. There are some people out there that have ulterior

motives, including slipping some form of a date rape drug in your drink. I have even heard cases of men consuming substances intended for their date.

Another caution is to not drink every drink that comes your way. At least drink a water between every few drinks.

16. Don't leave certain items in the sun.

The sun is so powerful things not directly exposed to the sun will still melt easily; such as in a hot vehicle. Liquids will evaporate or explode, pets will dehydrate, leather will become dangerously scorching, electronics can be severely damaged, etc.

Black attracts the sun and is prone to generate even more oven-like conditions. Tinting the windows of your car and using sun reflectors in the windows is a great way to keep the temperature down inside a car that is in the sun. This tip is extremely useful on the 120+ degree days.

17. Don't be rude to security.

This is a quick way to end your clubbing long before you are ready. If you are complaining and being disrespectful at the door of a nightclub, there is a good chance you will not even enter. Once you're in the door, you must continue to follow the policies of each venue. One small mistake can lead to being kicked out of the club, 86ed or even incarcerated.

18. Don't let Vegas get you down.

The last thing you want to do is become jaded. There is so much going on here it becomes difficult to keep up with everything. There are also many standards that must be met in order to keep a good reputation in Vegas. Keeping up with fashion trends, maintaining responsibilities, controlling spending impulses, and avoiding negativity can become very wearing on a person.

19. Don't step over the ropes.

The security obviously places these red ropes for some reason and they take people stepping over them very seriously. It may seem ridiculous and nerve racking, but you must wait for security to open the rope for you and follow their procedures if you want to pass go.

20. Don't get hooked.

Gambling, as well as other traditional Vegas activities, can become highly addictive. Remember that there are consequences for your actions, and habits can form very quickly.

Use your best judgment when choosing what you decide to get involved in.

Even when doing something good like giving a generous donation to a homeless person, by giving to all homeless people you could be left penniless.

21. Don't forget where you came from.

Perhaps you are just planning to visit Vegas, but it is all too easy to get distracted from your everyday responsibilities. Be sure to properly tend to important matters, such as your job, your spouse, your kids and your pets.

For someone living in the greater Las Vegas area, this tip simply implies that whether lady luck is or is not acting in your favor there are people & places that have shaped your life. It is important to take the time to appreciate them.

I still talk to my mom and grandma almost every day. I used to call because I felt I had to, but now it's just because I want to. It's not that I have to necessarily live in Ohio, but the daily call is a reminder that I cherish them no matter where I may be.

4

ARRIVING IN VEGAS

Regardless of your means of transportation, for most visitors the journey to Sin City is very exciting and somewhat stressful.

It seems as flights to Vegas have an entirely different operation all together. Even the announcers on the loud speaker have a hint of excitement in their voice. Although it may be common to hear, "Our destination is Vegas, baby," no one ever gets on a plane destined for Texas and hears, "this afternoon our destination is Houston, baby."

The passengers seem to be full of energy and ready for anything, except for those only headed to Las Vegas for a brief layover.

For those that will be traveling in a vehicle, bus, or even by train, a breathtaking scenic trip awaits you. The mountain views from any direction are simply amazing; however, these windy roads can be dangerous for drivers operating on little sleep or those with a limited attention span.

Whether a passenger or a driver, it is extremely vital to arrive with a reasonable amount of rest. Las Vegas is nonstop and the last thing you want to do is begin your visit feeling drained. However, once again I find that this is something that is easier for me to suggest versus follow my own advice.

This exciting city will exhaust you by entertainment, action and extreme heat from the dry desert conditions. Be sure to pack wisely, bring plenty of funding, and get plenty of rest before you get to Las Vegas.

Price comparison online on travel sites can save you large amounts of money. Be sure to check www.SinCitySurvivalGuide.com for savings and discounts on booking travel, accommodations, shows and attractions. Registering and signing up for a Players Card is also a fantastic way to save on hotel and food during your visit. Special offers will then be sent to your email alerting you of any specials or discounts.

WHERE TO STAY

Consider Las Vegas the Disney World for adults. Each person that visits Las Vegas has their own unique purpose for their journey, some more complex than others. Many will be visiting primarily for a conference or convention, in which case their accommodations will more than likely be predetermined by the business or group setting up this specific event.

Do you know how many conventions are in Las Vegas annually?
 …Find out in Chapter 18, 702 Trivia.

For nonbusiness related groups, ask when booking about discounts for multiple rooms whether you would like to stay at a hotel or other available accommodations. Families or friends with a large number of guests should consider renting a vacation home, timeshare or request a special group rate.

Those in search of "normal" accommodations, meaning visitors that are not here to party, have a much more difficult decision on their hands when it comes to deciding on which casino to stay at.

With so many choices for where to lay your head, it is important to choose a location that best fits the type of people you wish to be surrounded by. Also research in advance to take full advantage of all the features and amenities available at the location you decide on.

For those families visiting with children, a vacation home or family geared casino such as New York-New York, Circus Circus, Luxor, Excalibur or Treasure Island would be an ideal choice.

The Mandarin Oriental is as upscale as it gets. The service is 5 star and the decor reflects art, style and innovation. The entire block of City Center seems to excel at excellence and with their premiere real estate; the Mandarin is definitely top of the line.

There are a few hotels with similar names and some that are just located in confusing locations. Let me explain...

First of all, if you are looking for the Four Seasons or The Hotel, they are both located on the Mandalay Bay property.

The Signature at MGM Grand is a separate hotel from MGM Grand, which is still located on the MGM property. The Sky Lofts at MGM have hot tubs and a stunning view of the Strip.

Palms Casino consists of Fantasy Tower, Ivory Tower and Palms Pool Bungalows. Palms Place is adjacent, connected by an enclosed moving walkway just past the food court.

Traveling with family versus friends should be considered when deciding on staying at a hotel or casino that promotes a professional level of partying. This is especially critical during the calendar dates for adult themed events and conventions.

Insider Tip: The Hard Rock is the primary annual location for activities during the AVN Awards. (XXX)

LAS VEGAS HOTELS

Alliante Station
Aria
Artisan Boutique & Hotel
Bally's
Blue Green
Bellagio
Boulder Station
Cannery I & II
Caesars Palace
Circus Circus
Cosmopolitan
Cromwell
Encore
Excalibur
Fiesta Henderson
Fiesta Rancho
Flamingo
Four Seasons
Gold Coast
Golden Nugget
Green Valley Ranch
Hard Rock
Hooters Harrah's
Hilton Grande Vacations
Hyatt Place
LVH
Luxor
M
Mandalay Bay
Mandarin Oriental
Marriot
MGM Grand
Mirage
Monte Carlo
New York-New York
Palace Station
Palazzo
Palms
Palms Place Paris
Planet Hollywood
Orleans
Red Rock
Renaissance
Rio All-Suite Hotel & Casino
Riviera
Rumor Boutique & Hotel
Santa Fe Station
Silverton
SLS *Coming Soon*
South Point
Sunset Station
Suncoast Station
Stratosphere
The Signature
Texas Station
The Hotel
The Quad Treasure Island
Tropicana Trump
Tuscany
Vdara
Venetian
Wild Wild West
Wyndam
Wynn

5

ADAPTING TO YOUR SURROUNDINGS

Adjusting to the eccentric nexus of Sin City is a process that takes time to master.

Nevada's dry dusty climate is quite different than the conditions where most tourists are visiting. There are some precautions to consider when preparing for travel.

Vegas may have you may thinking you are the Energizer Bunny; however, without meeting your body's basic needs, you cannot keep going and going and going. The importance of food and H20 may not seem like a priority for most people with all the distractions and alternative options, but you should really consider making it a little more important for optimum results.

Sleep is something that is mandatory for your body to function properly. I know this may be a struggle since the casinos never close and the options you can choose from seem to be never ending.

JUST BECAUSE LAS VEGAS IS 24 HOURS DOES NOT MEAN YOU SHOULD BE TOO.

Perhaps those of you visiting cannot seem to get on a traditional time schedule, even if you are making a vigilant attempt at sleeping. Well, that could be due to the lack of clocks inside the casinos. Could it be true they want you to stay and spend every last dollar that you have? The fact that Las Vegas locals do not exactly operate on a 9-5 schedule may also play a part in your Vegas routine.

The heat and the partying can really take a toll on your body, so it is crucial to get the nourishment and rest you need to keep up with your planned itinerary. Staying hydrated is a necessity. You should always carry water with you when driving or walking a significant distance.

WARNING: HEADING DIRECTLY INTO THE HEAT WHEN SUFFERING FROM POST PARTY PAIN IS NOT THE BEST IDEA.

AVOIDING HANGOVERS

Prevention is key. Hangovers are common in Sin City and can best be avoided by drinking plenty of water while you are drinking, followed by even more water before you go to sleep.

A late night snack is a great way to soak up all the alcohol you have consumed throughout the night. With a limitless number of 24-hour restaurants and fast food options, this should not be a difficult task.

Ibuprofen or another form of pain reliever with a greasier food option the next day will have you feeling much better in no time.

A massage or day at the spa could also be excellent ways for coping with a hangover. If you wake up and realize that you are still drunk and the hangover has not quite kicked in yet, you have the option to simply keep drinking. By continuing to consume the alcohol, you are able to maintain a blood alcohol level that won't cripple your body & mind. Order a Mimosa with your breakfast & enjoy another day in paradise.

Another trending cure for the dreaded Sin City hangovers are oxygen bars. If you have been to Las Vegas in the last 10 years, you have probably noticed the influx of oxygen bars and buses that offer nutritious revitalizing shots with B12 and vitamins.

An oxygen bar takes the ambient air and absorbs all the nitrogen out and feeds you a flow of 85 percent to 95 percent oxygen. They also bubble the oxygen through a flavored liquid to provide an aroma, which is the same as aromatherapy.

Now there is even a mobile IV Rescue. This service gives you IV treatment to prevent serious hangovers. 619-252-5901

HYGIENE

When in need of a simple toiletry item such as a toothbrush or razor, simply call the front desk or housekeeping at almost any hotel.

Wash your hands as frequently as possible. Just as you touch things out of habit, so do all the visitors, who also touch the same door handles, rails, elevator buttons, etc.

As for hygiene, swimming in the pool at one of the "DayLife" parties, does not count as a shower.

Bring plenty of lotion and possibly a saline solution if you want to avoid dry skin and any difficulty with breathing.

If your eyes are itchy or irritated, you may need to use eye drops due to the dry and dusty climate. This could also be caused because in Las Vegas, smoking is legal inside the casino and clubs.

In shopping areas, retail stores and select restaurants there are some nonsmoking restrictions.

Also bring extra undergarments, as you will sweat more than normal during the months of extreme heat.

WEATHER

January: Day temperatures are somewhere around the mid-50s, but it does tend to drop quite a bit once the sun goes down. (Wearing layers of clothing is always a good choice.)

February: February is the cloudiest, windiest and wettest month, even though it still gets far less rain than the rest of the country.

March & April: These are great months to visit because although you may need a jacket at night, daytime you might be able to wear shorts.

May to mid-June: The weather begins to heat up and its time to break out the tank tops and bikinis as the summer heat approaches. The pools are usually open a week or 2 before Memorial Day but the holiday marks the official opening of the pools.

Mid-June to Mid-September: HOT. Some say it's a dry heat, but regardless when the temperature is reading over 100 degrees on a daily basis, the bottom line is...it's HOT!

Mid-September and October: These are the prime months to visit as it finally begins to cool down. The daytime and nighttime temperatures begin to differ more, the nights become chilly and windy. The pool parties slow down after Labor Day. By Halloween it is definitely too windy and too cool to be hanging out by the pool.

November: No more bikini weather as it begins to get much colder in general. It's still much warmer than other parts of the country, but probably time to put the shorts away. The winds begin to howl across the valley at night, making the dry desert extremely frigid.

December: This is one of our coldest months, and one of the few times of the year when checking the short-term forecast for weather updates could be a wise idea. The days are still manageable but the nights become bone chilling.

THE LAS VEGAS FORECAST

DRY HEAT?

Beating the heat can be very difficult in months such as August when temperatures rise above 120 degrees. The scalding conditions are often referred to as "dry heat," due to the lack of humidity, but no matter how you look at it there are a couple months that the weather can best be described as sizzling.

SUN DAMAGE

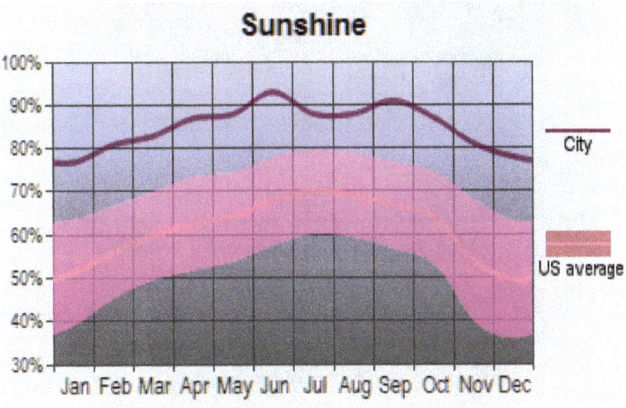

The sun's powerful rays can be harmful to your skin and vision. Visitors are encouraged to wear sunscreen. When your skin is not used to this type of sun exposure, sun block is vital. Looking like a lobster or getting sun poisoning can be avoided. Try spray tan for a darker skin tone.

STRONG WIND

Gusty winds and powerful lightning are also common for the local Vegas forecast.

CHANCE OF RAIN?

Typically it does not rain or snow very often in Vegas, however the last 2 years have seemed to produce more humid air than usual.

When it does rain, look out for flash flooding. Due to the dry earth, the rain is unable to soak into the ground and roadways are quickly covered when rain starts to fall.

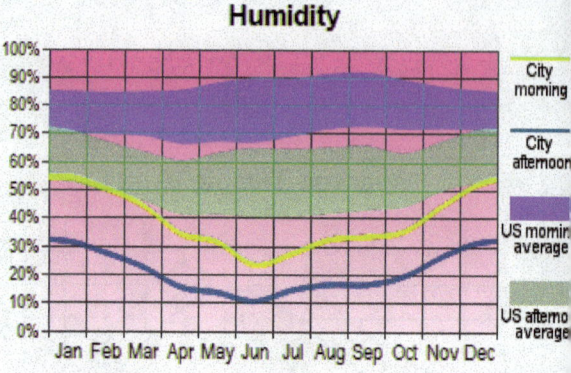

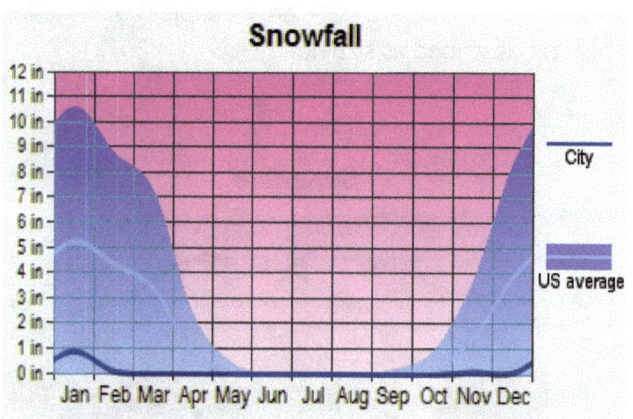

SNOW VS. DUST

Although there are not frequent snow or rainstorms, the Vegas Valley is prone to dust storms, which make it difficult to breath.

WEIRD WEATHER

The temperature drops tremendously at night on winter nights, especially in the desert where the wind chill can be extremely cold.

Oh and don't even get me started on how weird the clouds are here. Lol.

6

ENTERTAINMENT & DINING

As the Entertainment Capital of the World, Las Vegas has never-ending amount of entertainment options for almost anyone. Wether you are with a group or venturing out solo, there is always something to do in Sin City.

The Welcome to Las Vegas Sign is a great way to start off your trip to LasVegas. Found on the Southern end of the strip, this iconic sign has a red carpet and parking area for visitors to park and take photos.

The best views of the strip can be seen from a helicopter ride above the strip. Helicopter rides are also available to destinations such as Red Rock Canyon, Hoover Dam, and even the Grand Canyon. I went at sunset and have had a new appreciation of this beautiful city ever since.

Mandalay Bay offers a collection of art galleries and shopping, along with the House of Blues & Foundation Room.

The Shark Reef at Mandalay Bay is a unique activity. Mandalay Bay also has many art galleries, the House of Blues and the Michael Jackson Theater. Adjacent to Mandalay Bay are the Four Seasons & The Hotel.

The Luxor is another casino that is simply a work of art. The architecture and Egyptian garnishing are unlike anything else on the Strip. The buffet is amazing! I highly recommend it. You could see some magic while at the Luxor, by master magician Criss Angel or experience the Bodies Exhibit.

Located on the iconic corner where LVB crosses Tropicana, known as the 4 corners, is the Tropicana Hotel & Casino. The Tropicana will always carry itself as a respectable icon of Las Vegas with great accommodations.

If you are traveling with children, plan to make a stop at the arcade and medieval dragon show in Excalibur.

MGM is a posh super center of entertainment, hotel rooms & dining. The MGM hosts many annual events, rodeo shows and concerts. For years it has been renowned for its infamous pool parties at Wet Republic.

The roller coaster at New York-New York is a must ride! This is the perfect attraction for guests of any age, except for those with heart conditions, back problems, or who are pregnant. New York-New York also has some cool shops and restaurants that mimic the iconic NYC.

When it comes to high-class innovation, the new City Center exudes decadence and style. City Center consists of several modern buildings and casinos, such as Crystals Shopping, Cosmopolitan, Vdara, Mandarin Oriental, Aria, and Jockey Club.

City Center is equipped with top of the line technology and a vast selection of shops, theaters, nightclubs, casinos, restaurants and eateries.

The Monte Carlo has the out-of-the-box, family friendly show that is entertaining and very original, the Blue Man Group. There is also a well-known restaurant that sits directly on Las Vegas Blvd, Diablos. Minus 5 is a bar that lends you a coat at the door for a polar-like experience. Drink from an ice luge in an arctic like bar.

As you find yourself experiencing multiple cultures, you cannot pass up the French aspect of Las Vegas, found at Paris Hotel & Casino. Home to Gordon Ramsey's infamous "Hells Kitchen," along with several other exquisite dining options, you do not want to pass up your chance to receive a taste of France.

If you're ready to shop till you drop, try the Miracle Mile shops at Planet Hollywood, which offers a shopping experience that is definitely one of a kind. Planet Hollywood (PH) also offers posh accommodations and a variety of tasty eats. Shows such as Peep Show & the Vegas Comedy show are also fun attractions located at Planet Hollywood.

Bellagio's gardens, elegant trimmings, and infamous "O" fountain show are absolutely stunning. Bellagio has several exquisite restaurants such as Yellowtail and Hyde (which is also a nightclub). Bank is another premiere nightclub located inside Bellagio.

For those of you looking to shop, try the forum shops at the legendary Caesars Palace. Well known for its wedding chapel, Caesars offers a superior level of excellence. Dining options at Caesars are out of this world as well. Have a drink on Cleopatra's barge, Seahorse Lounge, Numb Bar, Galleria Bar, Spanish Steps or at the sensual Shadow Bar. Caesar's is also famous for it's Bocce Ball at Rao's and Sports Book.

The Garden of the Gods is the elegant pool oasis located at Caesars Palace.

The new Ferris wheel the "High Roller" is the tallest in the world at 550 feet; however, I have heard rumor that New York City is building a larger wheel as the Ferris frenzy continues.

Harrah's is an older casino and thus brings in an older demographic. The Flamingo would also fall under this generalization.

Another excellent attraction is the Gondola ride inside the Venetian. The ceiling of the Venetian grand canal shops is incredible. The Venice décor is definitely something everyone visiting Vegas should experience.

The Palazzo is adjoining to the Venetian and has stunning architecture, art, fountains and accommodations. Both Venetian and Palazzo are extremely close to the Sands Convention Center.

When it comes to class, there are a few other casinos playing the right cards, such as Wynn & Encore. With topnotch embellishments, unbelievable nightclubs, and 5 star restaurants the Wynn & Encore are 2 of the ritziest casinos in Vegas. The Wynn Espionage caters to the elite shoppers looking for high quality premiere shopping. The Wynn also has the lavish Ferrari dealership & showroom for you car enthusiasts.

The convention centers, such as the Las Vegas Convention Center and the Sands Expo Hall, are always booming with trade shows and industry professionals. LVH is the hub of activity when the convention halls are filled.

Double-decker buses offer 24-48 hour passes through Big Bus Tours. They also have the option for a Panoramic Night Tour.

FAMILY ATTRACTIONS

Laser tag, mini golf, tours and exhibits are available with more information on the Sin City Survival Guide website and mobile application.

For families visiting with children, the Thrill Rides located at the Stratosphere are a great activity with family appropriate fun to the extreme. The thrill rides include the Big Shot, X-Scream, Insanity, and SkyJump. The SkyJump is the scariest ride I can imagine, where you literally jump off of the Stratosphere.

The "Top of the World" restaurant spins slowly around while dining, providing a very unique dining experience.

The Adventure Dome at Circus Circus is a great family attraction, including its rides and Carnival Midway.

Don't miss the free shows that take place nightly, like the Volcano show at Mirage.

The exotic animals near the pool at Siegfried & Roy's Secret Garden and Dolphin Habitat at Mirage are activites for all ages.

Right next-door is the pirate show at Treasure Island, yet another remarkable free show that should be at the top of your to-do list, but it may be replaced by a shopping center by the time you read this book.

The Old Vegas and Fremont Street area is like a different era. Located in Downtown Las Vegas, the Fremont Street Experience offers free nightly shows featuring 12.5 million lights and 550,000 watts of amazing sound at VivaVision. Enjoy free concerts & special events all year. Show Times are 6pm, 7pm, 8pm, 9pm, 10pm, 11pm, 12am.

Saved the best for last, This is a MUST RIDE!
"Zip the Strip" is one of my absolute favorite tourist activities.

Price Guide for Show Listing

Under $50 $
$50-75 $$
$75-100 $$$
$100-150 $$$$
$150+ $$$$$

LAS VEGAS SHOWS & PRICES

Le Reve: The Dream (Wynn) $$$$$
O (Bellagio) $$$$$
Jersey Boys (Paris) $$

The Beatles (Mirage) $$$$
Human Nature: The Motown Show (Venetian) $$$
Blue Man Group (Monte Carlo) $$$
Ka Cirque Du Soleil (MGM) $$$
Mystere (Treasure Island) $$$
Absinthe (Caesars) $$$
Jabbawockeez (Luxor) $$$
PANDAI (Palazzo) $$$$
Penn & Teller (Rio) $$$
Michael Jackson ONE (Mandalay Bay) $$$
Rock Of Ages (Venetian) $$
Criss Angel Believe, Cirque Du Soleil (Luxor) $$$
V: The Ultimate Variety Show (Planet Hollywood) $
Zumanity, Cirque Du Soleil (New York New York) $$$
Country Superstars (Planet Hollywood) $
Legends In Concert (Flamingo) $$
Zarkana, Cirque Du Soleil (Aria) $$$
Divas Starring Frank Marino (Quad Resort) $$
Donny & Marie (Flamingo) $$$$
The Australian Bee Gees (Excalibur) $$
Evil Dead: The Musical (Planet Hollywood) $
Carrot Top (Luxor) $$
MAMMA MIA! $$

BOOK YOUR SHOW TICKETS AT
WWW.SINCITYSURVIVALGUIDE.COM.

WHERE TO EAT

When it comes to fine dining, grubbing out or trying some new cuisine, there is definitely a vast selection of restaurants and buffets to choose from. In fact, Las Vegas has some of the finest eateries in all the country and possibly the world. Chefs from around the globe visit Sin City to master and showcase their craft.

If you are trying for something healthier, Raw Fusion Foods is a great alternative. These raw food-based spice kits turn a simple salad into sensational super food. Find out more by going to www.rawfusionfoods.com.

The Fireside Lounge at the Peppermill. It is open 24 hours and is the legend when it comes to a late night dining experience where you can eat in a forest with fire and water fountains.

TOP 10 BUFFETS

1. Studio B at M Resort
2. Pharaoh's Feast at Luxor
3. Rio's Carnival World Buffet
4. Paradise Cafe at Fremont Street
5. The Buffet at Wynn
6. Bistro Buffet at Palms
7. Bellagio Buffet
8. Cravings at Mirage
9. Ports O' Call Buffet
10. Wicked Spoon at Cosmopolitan

7

OFF THE STRIP

Take some time to get off the beaten path and see what else Las Vegas and the nearby attractions have to offer.

If you have had enough of the casinos and are looking for something exciting to do, have no fear: there are many options to choose from.

The Hoover Dam is a staple for sightseeing near Vegas. This is a great location for families traveling with children in search of entertainment that is a bit more educational.

The Neon Boneyard is home to many of the original iconic neon signs used in Vegas. It is not open to the general public and typically it is necessary to call and schedule a tour or photo shoot.

Lake Mead is found in the area near the Hoover Dam but is also home of many water sport events and recreation. Lake Mead is the largest reservoir by volume in the United States according to the United States Bureau of Reclamation.

There are plenty of attractions to see off the busy strip of Sin City. The Las Vegas Motor Speedway is more than just a racetrack. This venue is also used for the Electronic Daisy Carnival (EDC) and for Christmas lights during the holidays.

Lake Las Vegas is another excellent choice for families or for those of you looking for a destination that is focused more on relaxation. Wine walks are a common event at this desert oasis.

The Springs Preserve is 180 acres of nature walks through a luscious landscape of fertile ground and wildlife.

For those of you looking to experience nature, Mt. Charleston or Red Rock are absolutely beautiful locations. Both options are gorgeous to drive through and offer activities such as hiking, rock climbing and rappelling.

Mt. Charleston is a refreshing retreat during the extremely hot summer months, due to its temperatures being significantly cooler. In the winter, visitors can ski and snowboard, making it a superb choice for any season.

Red Rock is a beautiful area great for hiking and climbing with a large number of climbing areas and trails. The summer gets very hot, so be sure to bring water with you to stay hydrated.

Red Rock Resort and Casino is located about 20 minutes from the strip but is a very family-friendly, upscale choice for visitors or locals looking for somewhere off the strip to dine or watch a movie.

Red Rock Lanes is the ultimate bowling experience. With a nightclub atmosphere and bottle service it is the perfect place to enjoy fun club-like experience without the crowds. It is 72 lanes of the most luxurious bowling in the country.

Off-road excursions are readily available for you to use dune-buggies, 4x4s, ATVs and more.

Bootleg Canyon Flight Lines allows you to fly over 8,000 feet of the canyon on a zi-pline in Boulder, NV.

Mesquite, Nevada is a resort destination just 80 miles north of Las Vegas that is a great getaway, although the secret of its beauty is getting out as it is rapidly growing.

Laughlin, Nevada offers a small western town atmosphere with casinos, entertainment and dining. Laughlin is home to some of the finest water recreation activities. It is also home of the Avi Resort & Casino, which borders 3 states (California, Arizona, & Nevada).

Bonnie Springs is a destination that makes it seem as if you have journeyed back in time. This Old Western tourist attraction near Blue Diamond is a great experience for all ages. You cannot miss the train at Bonnie Springs, "All aboard!" Choo-Choo!

The Grand Canyon is only a short drive away from Las Vegas, where you can walk on a glass bridge

over the canyon, helicopter over it or even ride a donkey down the walls and into the pit of this natural wonder.

Lake Havasu is a popular spring break destination known for its gorgeous scenery and serious boat parties.

Perfect for a day or weekend trip, Lake Tahoe offers skiing in the winter and outdoor activities in the summer.

VEGAS GOLF COURSES

GOLF

Surprisingly enough, Las Vegas is home to some absolutely "sinsational" golf courses.

If you are golfing in Vegas, realize that the grass is probably not going to be greener on the other side. More than likely, it is going to be the dry Nevada desert. The following list is compiled of the finest Las Vegas golf courses.

Rio Secco
Cascata Golf
Royal Links Golf Club
Desert Pines Golf Club
Bali Hai Golf Club
Alliante Golf Club
Las Vegas National Golf Club
Revere Golf Club
Bear's Best
Boulder Creek Golf Club
Callaway Golf Center
Eagle Crest
Legacy Golf Club
Painted Desert Golf Club
Siena Golf Club
TPC Las Vegas
Wild Horse Golf Club
Wynn Las Vegas Golf

8

BETTER SAFE THAN SORRY

The best way to solve any problem is… Prevention! Don't let the problem happen in the first place.

It is impossible to ignore the constant surveillance you are under most everywhere in the city. If it's not on camera, people still talk. If you are doing something you don't want anyone to know about, you have to ask yourself if you should be doing it at all? Remember: these tips are not intended to scare you, understand it is far better to be aware rather than aloof.

GENERAL ADVISORIES

A valuable key to avoiding dangerous and stressful situations is to know where everyone in your group is (maybe even implement the buddy system).

If a member of your party decides to go their own way, someone should know where they are headed and whom they are leaving with. Anything could happen.

It is always a good idea to plan ahead with a flexible strategy. The entertainment, music style, and atmosphere can change drastically each night even if you are at the same club. Check by calling the venue hosting whatever activities you plan to partake in and ask any questions you may have about the event; such as the featured entertainment, times, pricing or dress code.

When deciding on the length of your stay in Las Vegas, it is important to leave room for error. It is not uncommon for people to change their flight or decide to extend their stay.

IMPORTANT SAFETY REMINDERS

1. Smell before you drink.
2. Trust your instincts.
3. Double lock your hotel room.
4. If it sounds too good to be true, it probably is.
5. If it's none of your business, stay out of it. There are some things that are just better off left alone.
6. Wear a condom; you never know what you are protecting yourself from.
7. Prepare for the worst & hope for the best. Preparation is key for success.
8. For the most part, keep it real because being fake can only get you so far before the truth comes out.
9. Read the fine print. Many times people ignore the details and look only at the prize, finding themselves responsible for much more than what they had originally anticipated.
10. If you are unsure, ask questions. This goes for almost everything.
11. If you are concerned for your safety, buy some mace or a stun-gun from one of the local spy stores.
12. Know your exits.

Remember: these tips are not intended to scare you, understand it is far better to be aware rather than aloof.

Some say "rules are made to be broken;" however, there are some rules in Vegas that must be followed.

"Vegas was built on exploiting weaknesses. Know your weaknesses."
-Justin Inabinett

WHETHER YOU ARE A LOCAL OR JUST VISITING IT IS ALWAYS A GOOD IDEA TO MEMORIZE A FEW PHONE NUMBERS. THIS IS JUST A PRECAUTION IN CASE AN EMERGENCY SITUATION ARISES, SUCH AS GETTING WASTED OR DOING SOMETHING OFF THE WALL RESULTING IN JAIL. YOU DON'T EXACTLY GET TO KEEP YOUR PHONE IF YOU'RE GOING TO BE ARRESTED.

GAMBLING

If you choose to take your chances at the casinos, be sure you only gamble with funds that you consider spending money. Also be sure you know the rules of the game and policies of the casino.

A great game for beginners is Blackjack because it has better odds than the other table games and is far less complicated than games such as Roulette or Craps.

There are several different types of versions of each game, such as 3 card, 4 card and 5 card poker.

There are also differences in the number of decks being used per table. Check to see if it is single deck or multi-deck if you want to increase your chances of winning.

When using a slot machine, check the payouts and how many coins are required to play to actually win.

Use Table Etiquette. You cannot be on your phone and be cautious with the use of profanity at the tables. If you are a rookie, let the dealer know that so they can give you as much direction as they are permitted to.

High Limit Gambling is an area designated to those with funds that can support a large bet per hand. Consider it the first class of the casino.

BEHIND THE WHEEL

Driving in Vegas is like playing sports; offense & defense are required behind the wheel.

The main strip of Las Vegas is filled with glittering lights and endless entertainment. Nonetheless, this can all be very distracting while driving.

Always remember to turn your lights on. There is not a night that goes past that I do not see someone make this mistake. Focus on the road and please stay awake at the wheel.

Watch for pedestrians. Even though the light is green you could easily still turn a group of tourists into a crosswalk buffet. If you're on empty, don't risk running out of gas; just stop at the next gas station.

Be prepared to deal with construction...Lots of it. Not only is this challenging due to the obvious risks involved, but also because the patterns of the cones and lines on the road are constantly being redirected.

Have a designated driver and pay attention. When planning your trip or even if you live here, keep in mind a taxi is cheaper than DUI.

Remember where you park. Text yourself which casino, parking level or possibly even take a photo if your short-term memory is not up to par. There are also helpful little cards in most casinos near the elevator with the casino name & the level you are on.

Do not assume that anyone in a parking lot is a valet attendant. My good friend Leora almost gave her car to someone random in a parking lot until I stopped her. She learned a valuable lesson that day.

Tip for locals: If you try to be a creature of habit by parking in the same place at each casino, the chances of you losing your car decrease greatly.

Have a backup plan... If you find yourself without any other transportation, you can view the transportation route and schedule at www.rtcsouthernnevada.com.

UNDERSTANDING THE FLOW OF TRAFFIC

The Greater Las Vegas area includes the nearby towns of Henderson, Summerlin, Primm, and of course the heart of Las Vegas, which is the central area where the majority of hotels & casinos are located.

The area known as the spaghetti bowl intersection is where the I-15, I-95, I-515 connect and reroute. This area is known for heavy rush hour traffic and countless accidents, so buckle up and drive on the defense. Please don't be one of those cowardly drivers and drive like your grandmother (sorry, no offense Nana). Drive close to the speed limit and keep up with the flow of traffic. Stay off the cell phone if you are in the driver's seat.

Here is another map of Las Vegas and the surrounding areas for those of you that may be directionally challenged.

9

THINK OF THE SAVINGS

One thing that is commonly overlooked in Las Vegas is the ability to save money by planning ahead.

Let's start with visitors... Frequent Flyer and Rapid Rewards' points add up. Keep track of your special offers so you can visit Vegas again with your earned credit.

There is power in numbers. For the most part you can save money by booking reservations as a group. As it happens, there is a great deal of discounts for visitors and locals at your disposal if you simply ask. Obviously this is true with bottle service at nightclubs, but also with accommodations, attractions and tours.

This is especially important to consider if you plan to visit during a holiday weekend. The cost of show tickets, club admission, hotel rentals and various other forms of entertainment, will continue to increase based on availability. Planning ahead is imperative for those of you with limited funds available. Book show tickets on the Sin City Survival Guide website for big discounts.

Cash in on the available FREEBIES. There are many giveaways you could be eligible for at the casinos, so be sure to sign up for a player's card and listen for special offers.

Many casinos will send out promotional mail with free vouchers and coupons that are extremely generous. Sign up for a Player's card. Typically, you can apply for them while gambling or at the concierge desk.

Free drinks are offered to those that are gambling at most of the casinos. Sometimes it is only at select machines, but they do exist. ;)

Note to self: They charge a lot for the contents of the mini fridge! It is far more cost effective to buy your necessities and snacks from any grocery/convenience/liquor store that is not directly on the Strip or in a casino. There may be resort fees added to your room charges so read the fine print.

SHOP TILL YOU DROP?

When it comes to shopping in Sin City, luxury and style are evident, with a multitude of shops and boutiques to choose from. If you are a big spender, there is a wealth of high-end stores that feature extravagant jewelry and designer brands inside most of the casinos and at our local malls.

Whether you have cheap or expensive taste, there are definitely plenty of high-end stores that will amaze even the biggest shopping addict. If shopping is what you want, Vegas has more than you could imagine.

High-end Shopping

Crystals
Grand Canal Shoppes at Venetian & Palazzo
Forum Shops at Caesars Palace
Wynn Espionage
Miracle Mile Shops

Casino Boutiques, Jewelers and stores with handmade fashions & accessories are a great place to find a special gift for anyone. After a day at a pool party or spa, a shopping escapade is guaranteed to put a smile on anyone's face.

Shopping Malls

Town Square
The Galleria Mall
Meadows Mall
Fashion Show Mall
Local Secrets

Outlet shopping

Fashion Outlets of Las Vegas (FOLV)
Las Vegas Premium Outlets North
Las Vegas Premium Outlet South

Factory Outlet Malls are an ideal place to find great deals on discounted or out of the ordinary products.

One of my personal favorite places to shop is the Fantastik Indoor Swap Meet. Located off Sahara & Decatur Ave, they have everything…tons of cool gadgets, tools, art, clothing, accessories, hats, purses, luggage, plants, furniture, lighting, pets and makeup and even a farmer's market. I love playing dress-up and Vegas Girl Wigs is a necessity. Everything is better in a costume…well almost everything.

10 WAYS TO SAVE

1. Special offers are up for grabs for the majority of businesses in Vegas. This means for those who are: military, seniors, locals, and students, to name a few.
2. If you are looking for cheap show tickets, try going through hthe Sin City Survival Guide website, which offers show descriptions, entertainment options, and viewing times.
3. By signing up for Players Club cards and Membership rewards at most all casinos, there are even more savings at your disposal. Some casinos even offer free slot play just for signing up.
4. Read the menus carefully at restaurants and be sure to inquire about specials and promotions. Many buffets have hours that qualify for reduced admission.
5. Hitting up a happy hour is another great way to save on food and drinks.
6. Go for the group discount or buy in quantity.
7. Buy a bottle instead of wine by the glass. This is also valid for nightclubs, which I will explain later in the VIP Clubbing chapter.
8. Grab a coupon book. There are plenty of stands with brochures & coupon books in most taxis, casinos, hotels, tourism centers, or online.
9. Barter! Everything is negotiable.
10. Set a budget and stick to it.

OUT OF CASH $

If at some point, you find yourself down on your luck and without a buck, a great resource to make some quick cash is by going to Labor Ready or go to Craigslist and see what temp work is available in the paid gigs section. This goes for men &

women. They provide work ranging from modeling to yard work, convention shows and everything in between.

When I first moved here, I found myself strapped for funds and would go online and say, "What's up Craig?"

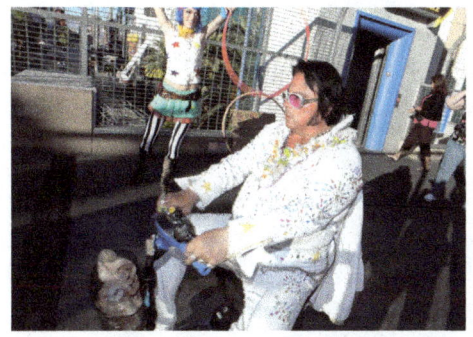

Be aware that there may be some ads that are scams online, so try researching the business before beginning work.

Maybe you could try cashing in some of your assets at Pawn Stars (as seen on TV

Who knows, maybe you have something you did not realize was worth a small fortune.

There are also many places that will accept your Gold or unwanted jewelry, such as the Gold Guys.

Another option is to stand in front of a Home Depot and get your work boots ready. There should be others out there as well, ask them to coach you. There is always a chance you could win big at the casino.

If all else fails you could always use your best talent and create your own street performance. However, you may need a permit or you could be fined or even thrown in jail. Licenses can be obtained by visiting: www.nevada.gov/Apply/licenses.html.

ALL YOU NEED IS HOPE. WHERE THERE IS A WILL, THERE IS A WAY.

10

GIRLS VS. BOYS

In Vegas, your gender makes a big difference when it comes to almost everything. What is below the belt has a serious impact on your treatment at almost all venues. Girls enjoy the good life. Guys have it rough. Sad but true, that is unless you're a man with money or a remarkable personality.

TIPS FOR THE LADIES

Sin City is the perfect location for a girls getaway weekend, bachelorette party, or even to celebrate a divorce. Vegas is full of possibilities for creating the ideal girls vacation, from premiere shopping to five star spas.

Accommodations such as suites, penthouses or rental condos can turn an ordinary trip into a female version of the Hangover movie. Prices may vary but it can be a great investment when executed properly.

Depending on when you visit Sin City, there are seasonal suggestions to consider. If your trip is during the months of March until October, you will more than likely want to check out one of the city's epic pool parties over the summer.

If you have not heard about the balls to the wall brunches that are held during the colder months, ladies this is your chance to party like a grandma gone wild or a stripper gone apeshit.

Do not be alarmed when rounding up everyone for an event suddenly turns into what seems like herding cats. With so many distractions it is seemingly impossible to keep a group of 3 or more girls on the same agenda for a significant amount of time.

BACHELORETTES

For those of you bachelorettes that are about to get married, I wish you the best of luck in love and bless your marriage with happiness, security, trust and compassion. See only love. -Rev. Tiff

In Vegas, bachelor & bachelorette parties can get a little out of control, so consider this...

If you are worried about someone seeing what you are up to, then chances are you probably should not be doing it at all. (That goes for bachelors too!)

Personally if I was going to go to Vegas for my bachelorette party, I would consider coming up with some terms with your fiancee before the trip for what is or is not acceptable. This way there is an understanding on what you are getting yourself into.

GIRLS NIGHT OUT

For you friskier felines, there are male reviews that are perfect for sisterly celebrations & special occasions, for example; Chippendales, Men of Sapphire, OG's male review, Thunder from Down Under, American Storm, etc.

You could also partake in a pole dancing class or arrange for a professional Vegas photo shoot.

Don't forget to do some strategic gambling gals! This is a city that encourages men to spend big on sexy girls. Always carry yourself with confidence and have fun! It's Vegas Baby!

LOCAL LADIES

If you're a local female and you are still paying for club entry, you must not get it.

If you are a female that is not a local, let me explain to you how to make the most of your clubbing experience. No matter what the size (or shape) of your group may be. Your best bet is to find a VIP host to guide you.

Hot babes with a Nevada ID can benefit from the perks of their Vegas residency by getting to know some hosts at the larger nightclubs, which can provide your group of 6-8+ ladies a free comped dinner or a free bottle.

WHAT TO WEAR

The good news is that Vegas is similar to London's fashion where pretty much anything goes if you are simply out and about. However, if you're going out to a night club, you may have to step it up a notch.

Women ready to hit the town and enjoy some of the city's world-renown nightclubs, let me remind you to wear comfortable shoes and dress to impress. Expect to see many extremely high heels, eyelashes, super small bikinis and boob jobs.

Choose a purse that you can carry without getting tired or having the feeling of carrying something heavy around.

Try to limit your "slutty" attire and accessories to only 1 article at a time. Class and Trash are only a few letters off.

"The general rule is, you don't want to pull a Pretty Woman."
-Skyler Haze

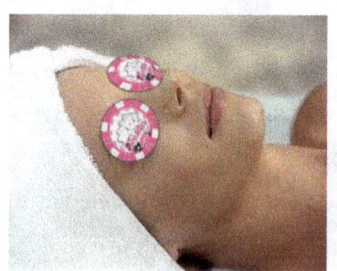

RELAX

Maybe none of this sounds like any fun to you at all. Well, sorry to raise your blood pressure. Maybe you should try a massage, facial, manicure, pedicure, spray tan or just a refreshing day at the spa.

TOP SPAS IN LAS VEGAS

1. The Spa at Mandarin Oriental
2. Qua Bath & Spa at Caesars Palace
3. Spa Bellagio
4. Imperial Health & Spa
5. Spa by Mandara at Paris Las Vegas
6. Spa Mandalay
7. The Spa @ Trump
8. A Touch of Las Vegas Day Spa
9. The Spa & Salon at Aria
10. The Spa and Salon at Encore
11. The Bathhouse at Mandalay Bay
12. Canyon Ranch SpaClub at Venetian
13. Drift Spa at Palms Place
14. ESPA at Vdara
15. Four Seasons at Four Seasons
16. Glow at Tropicana

ADVICE FOR THE FELLAS:

I hate to be the bearer of bad news, but where Las Vegas is a financial paradise for the ladies, I cannot say the same for the guys. These are crucial things every guy should know before coming to Vegas.

Expect to pay, most everywhere actually... Lets start with lunch + tip + dinner +tip + club entry at any nightclub + tip + drinks +tip + drinks for girls you meet + tip + fast food after (remember this will help you tons the next day) + gambling + taxi + tip + shows + tip + strip clubs +$$$$$TIP$$$$$$ + Anything (it's Vegas) = $$$$$$$$$$

What is the message behind this equation? Understand guys, you will be paying a significant amount more than women, especially if your group consists of mostly guys. So bring plenty of money and don't spend it all at once. Set yourself a daily limit and stick to it, unless you have unlimited funds.

Vegas can set the scene for some awesome guys trips as well, whether it is for a convention, bachelor party, or sporting event. I mean come on, I think everyone has seen at least one of the Hangover movies. Things get CRAZY here.

Thats right.... CRAZY! So guys, why not shoot some guns at one of the incredible shooting ranges or try racing exotic cars (or at least rent a fun car for the day or hour).

Or if you think that you are not ready for a sports car, maybe you could try a scooter.

As a last resort, there is go cart racing.

SHOOTING RANGES

Let's say you love guns. Well, so does Vegas. The following is a list of local shooting ranges. Just don't go shooting your eye out. ;)

The Gun Store
The Range 702
American Shooters
Guns & Ammo Garage
Presidential Club
Machine Gun Experience
Machine Guns Vegas

GOING OUT WITH THE GUYS

At the clubs, it may seem totally unfair that you have waited for over an hour in line, then 5 hot girls walk up and they open the ropes right up for them, while handing them free passes.

If you are with a group of all guys, your best bet is to grab at least couple of girls to walk in with and ask for bottle service. Because by the time you pay for entry and each buy 2 or 3 drinks, it's all going to cost close to the same anyway.

No matter how unfair you feel you're being treated, don't make enemies with the security or people at the door.

If you are complaining or getting smart, this is not funny to them, even if you may think you're the boss (or a boss if you're hood) the security will toss you out of the club, possibly 86 you or worse...they call Metro and you end up downtown.

Don't forget the strip clubs. The Spearmint Rhino and Sapphire are well known as 2 of the best strip clubs in the country. (The Strip Club Listing is a few chapters away, please see Chapter 13-After Hour Power)

GET DISCOUNTS AND MORE INFO AT WWW.SINCITYSURVIVALGUIDE.COM.

WHAT TO WEAR

Dress to impress because this is a city where your wardrobe does make a difference (yes this means guys too).

When in doubt wear a button down shirt at least and if you simply add a Sports Coat, that's the look you should probably go for.

Most importantly, bring dress shoes when you come to Vegas! Please!

I say go for a look that is fun. Even if you don't get in, or get thrown out, at least your outfit will keep you in a positive mood and make it that much easier for you to make some new friends.

WHEN GOING OUT BOYS, JUST SAY NO TO

1. No bad attitudes.

2. No droopy jeans.

3. No T-shirts-especially plain white.

4. No oversized chains that are bigger than one for your pet.

5. No Flip Flops.

6. No shorts at night-you gotta sweat it out....

7. No grizzly bear chest hair. I saw this guy at Wet Republic last year and his chest hair was so long and thick + matching back hair that we all thought he was wearing a vest at first...eww... that image is permanently engraved in my head....

8. No empty wallets. Bring at least some cash.

VESTS?

Vests should be worn on a case-by-case basis. Some guys can pull it off, some can't.

When in doubt, get a second opinion because this can also be used a great conversation starter.

"Expressing yourself through fashion should be effortless, never do too much."
-Pretty Rickey

HATS?

For the most part, hats should be worn with the understanding that you may or may not be returning home with it. Usually, if you are going out to a club I do not advise it, because it can easily get lost or you may go to a venue that does not allow hats.

My experience has been that at some point in the night, you will decide to take it off, at which point you will be stuck carrying it around.

I am a fan of hats though. So call ahead to see verify the dress code and use your own judgement on wearing a hat while clubbing.

11

VIP CLUBBING

There is going out to a nightclub ... and then there is going out to a nightclub in Las Vegas. Sin City is #1 in the United States when it comes to VIP clubbing!

PERHAPS SOME OF YOU MAY BE WONDERING,

"WHAT IS THIS GUEST LIST AND HOW DO YOU GET ON ONE?"

Well, this can be difficult for visitors, but my best advice is to try social media, call the venue directly or find a host or promoter that is willing to add your name to their list for comped or reduced entry.

For Locals, check the local nightlife magazines and social networks to find out what events are coming up that you may be interested in. Most clubs offer free or comped admission to those with a Nevada ID. Your ID makes a HUGE difference at the door whether you are male or female.

Another option is to register with that particular club online or at one of the Vegas Club Photo sites or at SinCitySurvivalGuide.com.

"Be sure to pick up the current issue of the local nightlife magazines or visit them online for a comprehensive listing of nightclubs with a breakdown of celebrity appearances, performers,
   DJ's and most importantly which genre of music is offered". -Danielle Moschella

BOTTLE SERVICE

Bottle service is definitely the way to go when visiting any club. First of all, you will not have to wait nearly as long in line and the price will include cover. In addition, you will now have a waitress and are able to avoid the lines at the bar. By the time you pay cover and buy drinks, it's all going to be the same price anyway.

Most importantly, you have somewhere to sit down! If you are with any girls, their feet are 99% going to hurt at some point. It is better to have a seat ready for them, rather than end your night early.

Next let's give you the scoop on the chain of command at the door. This should remain fairly accurate for most topnotch clubs.

1. The Promoter- an employee of the nightclub easily mistaken for the independent host. The independent host is someone that has an agreement with either the club or another host, which allows them exclusive privileges. This would be the person in the casino walking up next to you in the casino saying, "So hey, where are you going tonight? Ah well you should check out my club, its just right over there. Take this pass or wristband, and just say my name at the door. Tell them you know me and its all good. Ya feel me?"
   If you are considering entering the club, just take the bracelet because....
   A. It may help you later.
   B: They are going to continue to badger you until you agree to take it anyway.
2. The Door guy- great person to know, even if you have to buy their friendship. Slipping them a $20-$100 bill could save you hours of waiting. Furthermore after a few consistent good tips, they suddenly remember who you are and you are welcomed back with no wait at all. Ask for their business card, shoot them a text letting them know you are going to be headed to their club. This way they will be looking for you and it's much easier to get their attention.
3. The Host/VIP Host- This is definitely someone who can assist you greatly in avoiding the line and getting in free. The hosts holds the power of the guest list.

4. Management- The management team may or may not be visible at the door but typically can be available upon proper request.
5. Owner- Chances are the owner is not going to be at the door of most nightclubs. Most often they are not present, so be leery of people saying they falsely own the club.
6. Security- The security has different methods for handling the door at every club. At some clubs, their presence may simply act as precautionary warning for anyone in line to show respect to hosts and follow the basic club rules.

In other cases, their intent is to search every pocket, container, zipper and item you are trying to carry in the club with you. If they happen to find something they consider contraband; such as, lipgloss, gum, perfume, candy, eye drops, cameras, all liquids, prescription drugs etc. they will make you throw it away. Any weapons or nonprescription/illegal drugs, and you will be denied entry and you may be entering a visit with Metro instead.

The strangest thing I have ever seen anyone attempt to smuggle into a venue was when I watched security find a rubber duck in the back of a girl's bikini bottoms.

---

*The Bathroom Attendant
The female and male attendants in the restrooms don't have a counter of hairspray, cigarettes, body spray, candy, etc. for you to take for free, you have to tip if you take.
*In the club restrooms, you can only enter one at a time into the stalls. No one is going to buy into your story of how your friend is going to help you take a leak.

All these guidelines for the clubs may have you feeling intimidated and wondering if it's even worth it. Well your chances are better since you were smart enough to read this book. Preparation is key, so fun is easy if you know what your doing and you have a general idea of what to expect. At most clubs in Vegas, they do not play the same style of music every night. There is a simple solution, call ahead or check online to be sure that your not walking into a Tiesto performance expecting Lil Wayne (even if you go to that club every time you visit).

LEGENDARY EVENTS

On any given night, there are events, contests, and parties taking place in Vegas that are so incredible it could be the best time of your life.

Costume contests are my favorite, but I am convinced they are rigged for the most part. I mean seriously, I brought special fx (fake snow) for the Snow Bunny contest and had brought a ton of girls (that usually helps), yet was defeated by a girl that is not even smiling? Gotta be rigged.

Las Vegas hosts some of the world's most legendary parties annually, topping that list has got to be EDC.

Electronic Daisy Carnival (EDC) is the annual electronic music festival held every June at the Las Vegas Motor Speedway. Just about every major DJ in the world is on the roster for this colossal dance fiasco. Fireworks, carnival rides, special FX and some of the most elaborate stages you can imagine are the cause of this party selling out of tickets within days of going on sale each year. With over 250,000 people in attendance, this is one party you have to experience for yourself.

HOLIDAY WEEKENDS

Holiday celebrations on the Strip are unforgettable with fireworks along with a flood of tourists. However, I will give you a word of advice; expect to wait and expect to pay.

I am not saying do not visit during holidays, just keep in mind it is going to be at least twice as expensive on a holiday weekend, and the lines will be twice as long for
almost everything.

*This includes leaving extra time for travel, whether it is via flight, taxi or your usual route home for those of you whom are residents to the Greater Las Vegas area. If you are one of the many which chose to drive to and from California during peak hours on holiday weekends, I am sure you are used to traffic and there will be plenty of it. if you plan on taking the I-15 be sure to leave yourself an extra 3-6 hours for traffic during holidays.

Typically, a valid Nevada ID card can get you a long way in Vegas, but as I mentioned before Sin City runs on a sliding scale of gray. With that said, holiday weekends are one of the only times that even locals are forced to pay cover for door entry at pool parties and nightclubs.

73

NIGHTCLUB LIST

New in 2013, located at MGM, Hakkasan opened the doors of its 80,000 square foot, five-story restaurant and club complex, making it the largest club in the Nation. According to Forbes, the build out cost a whopping $100 million dollars to construct. If that sounds expensive, try paying the tab for the club's entertainers, such as Tiesto or Calvin Harris, who are getting paid $200,000 per night.

Beacher's Comedy Madhouse just opened a nightclub at MGM in January 2014, which draws quite an eclectic crowd of characters guaranteed to make you smile.

Mandalay Bay recently opened the 38,000 square foot mega club, Light, in summer 2013. Light is the world's first nightclub to integrate Cirque du Soleil and Electronic Dance Music (EDM), featuring international DJs with special FX. The new club also included the addition of a new day club called Daylight. Weekly on Wednesdays the pool becomes a nightclub referred to as Eclipse, which has an Ibiza appeal to it.

Foundation Room and MIX have some of the best views of the Strip, as the bar/lounge towers over Vegas from high on top of the Mandalay Bay towers.

Located at the Cosmopolitan, Marquee is one of my personal favorite nightclubs providing, in my opinion, the best sound system in the city. With 3 rooms of sound and an elaborate pool, Marquee is a well designed maze of advanced lighting and special FX combined with live performances from entertainers and DJs.

Cosmo is also home to the Chandelier Bar, which is the most elaborate piece of bling art I have ever laid eyes upon.

Aria has several nightclubs including, Haze, The Deuce and Gold Lounge.

When it comes to maintaining an ongoing reputation of excellence, XS holds the title for the highest annual revenue in the city, $60 million per year. XS is known for it's outstanding service, dance floor, bottle service, card tables and pool.

Surrender/Encore Beach Club (EBC) is a day and nightclub that features some of the best DJs and performers in the world. The venue is built with cabanas around a gorgeous pool that has walkways that connect each side along with floating lily pads, used for bottle service during their pool parties.

Tao Nightclub, located in the Venetian is Asian inspired, featuring a 20 foot statue of Buddah, an infinity edge pool, private "sky boxes" and 40 foot terrace. There are 2 features Tao offers that no other club in Vegas does: the beautiful girls that lay in bathtubs during the club hours and bathroom doors that steam when locked to block, rather than the standard bathroom door.

The Rock house is found at the Venetian, designed as edgy and Rock n Roll themed.

The V Bar is a lounge also in the Venetian and was voted "Best Hotel Bar."

Lavo is well known for its ridiculous brunches that serve champagne and glowsticks. They are also serving incredible food at

their restaurant and bottles at their nightclub. This club encourages "party rock" attire and all things glow, so if you love EDM and can appreciate being handed goggles at the door, this a fun place to go.

Body English at the Hard Rock is a nightclub and after hour venue that has a lowered dance floor that reminds me of a ballroom. It has excellent lighting and a steam machine, I was lucky enough to operate on a few occasions.

Moon at the Palms is a great club for those looking to dance under the open night sky and enjoy an amazing view without being pushed or waiting in lines like some of the bigger nightclubs.

Ghostbar Night/Day club is also at the Palms with a killer view that is downright frightening as you can stand on a glass pane over 50 stories above the street.

Bellagio has several gorgeous venues such as; Lily Bar, Hyde and the Bank.

Tryst is a nightclub inside the Wynn that has a huge waterfall and high-end bottle service. Dress code is strictly enforced.

Pure nightclub is well known for its consistent celebrity guests, Pussycat Dolls performers and rooftop dance floor.

Fizz elevates nightlife at Caesars Palace with high-end champagne, couture cocktails and fine art photography.

For a dance under the Eiffel Tower, don't miss Chateau inside Paris, where you have a breathtaking view of the Strip from literally inside the tower itself.

Mirage includes King Ink and 1 Oak Nightclub.

The Beatles's Revolution at the Mirage is more of a chill lounge that welcomes an older demographic.

Krave is the #1 Gay Nightclub in the country.

Piraña also caters to the Gay community located near the airport.

Voodoo at Rio has an unbelievable view of the Strip with multi levels of dance floors.

NIGHTCLUBS OFF THE STRIP

Blue Martini at Town Square Shopping Center is a great place for locals to grab a cocktail.

If you are a fan of country music, Stoney's is the place to be for a boot scooting good time. On Thursdays you can even participate in the Bulls & Bikinis contest, where you can bull ride in your bikini and even win some cash.

Another choice is Elixir in Green Valley.

Tacos & Beer is an off the Strip bar and lounge with a restaurant, but their specialty is artisanal tacos and craft beer.

Oracle Mansion caters to the Latin community with 2 rooms of sound.

DOWNTOWN NIGHTLIFE

Frankie's Tiki Room
Double Down Saloon
Beauty Bar
Downtown Cocktail Room
The Laundry Room
The Velveteen Rabbit
The Griffin
Don't Tell Mama
Fremont Street Experience
Atomic Liquor Store and Bar
Insert Coins
Artifice
Vanguard Lounge
Common Wealth
Dino's
The Lady Silvia Mermaid's
Mob Bar
Mingo Kitchen & Lounge
Snick's Place
Hogs & Heifers
Luna Rossa
Brass Lounge
Talk of the Town
Mickie Finnz
The Beat Coffeehouse
Courthouse Bar & Grill
Bar 46
Badlands Saloon
Las Vegas Country Saloon
Rush Lounge
LJ Bar & Grill
Saturday Night Stomp
Pulse Nightclub
Barley Pops
Drink & Drag Lounge

12

TOOLS FOR THE POOLS

In Vegas, clubbing is not just for nightlife. Here, tourists and locals keep the club pumping in the sunshine as well. These extraordinary pool parties have become referred to as DayLife. Celebrities, Performers, and DJs will continue the party all day at pools located inside the premiere casinos & hotels on the Strip.

POOLS THAT PARTY

DRAIS @ CROMWELL
WET REPUBLIC @MGM
ENCORE BEACH CLUB/SURRENDER @ ENCORE
REHAB @HARD ROCK
DAYLIGHT/ECLIPSE @ MANDALAY BAY
LIQUID @ARIA
TAO BEACH @VENETIAN
DITCH FRIDAY @PALMS
MARQUEE DAY CLUB @COSMO
THE ARTISAN
TROPICANA
AZURE @PALAZZO
GARDEN OF THE GODS @ CAESARS PALACE
SAPPHIRE POOL CLUB
DREAM @ M CASINO
GOLDEN NUGGET POOL
VOODOO BEACH @ RIO

Do not be surprised when you are searched at the door and charged a cover fee of $20-100+ just to enter.

POOL ATTIRE

How small is too small for swim wear?

In Sin City there is no such thing as too small! Skimpy and sexy define the bikinis worn by most Vegas Locals at DayLife parties.

When deciding on pool attire, yes girls do wear heels to the pool here, even I have done it on occasion. The thought of wearing stilettos in the sand may sound like torture, but beauty is pain and if you want to be VIP then you have to dress the part.

For those of you just visiting, it's much more acceptable to wear the flip flops and save your feet the torture until party time.

Do not forget your sunscreen. Water is also very important when spending the day out in the sun, so drink plenty of it, even if it is between alcoholic beverages.

As for guys, you can wear a speedo at most pools; however in my opinion this is a tough look to pull off unless you have an incredible body or you are from a foreign country.

You do need to wear a shirt to these locations to walk through the casino and hang onto it so that you can properly exit the topless pool as well. Topless pools typically have a slightly higher cover at door with bottle service options available.

TOPTIONAL POOLS
(TOP OPTIONAL)

THE BEACH @ MANDALAY BAY
BARE POOL @ MIRAGE
CAESARS PALACE
STRATOSPHERE ARTISAN
RIO
SIMON
SAPPHIRE

THE SEXIEST POOL PARTY

When it comes to babes in bikinis, there is one pool party you don't want to miss. The Vegas Hot 100 is one of the hottest pool parties of the summer, held at the legendary Wet Republic at MGM Grand Hotel & Casino.

THE WILDEST POOL PARTY

The craziest pool parties or any party for that matter is going to be a locals party. Industry locals always seem to make their way to the center of the action.

Courtesy of Universal Pictures.

13

AFTER HOUR POWER

The first rule of thumb is if you plan on pulling an all-nighter, or think it may be a strong possibility, bring sunglasses!

Whenever you decide to call it a night or at least take a break from whatever activities you choose to become involved in, realize that the sun is going to be waiting for you, stronger and brighter than it seemed to be the day before. Sunglasses are an essential for night owls and all night party people.

For those of you wondering, "What is after hours?" let me elaborate. After hours is a term used to refer to clubs that open after midnight and operate on a time schedule for night owls. In Vegas these venues play mostly electronic music and cater to a party-friendly demographic.

Life in the desert is all about adapting to your surroundings, thus some people begin running on different sleep patterns. This behavior is not only caused by excessive partying, but also by boiling temperature during the day. The nights become cooler and there is usually a breeze, so people want to make the nights longer.

IF YOU LOVE TO PARTY, THIS IS THE CITY TO BE IN.

Las Vegas is one of the only cities I have ever been to where people literally start their night at after hours around 3-4am, even sunrise. Some of you may be thinking, "Really?" Yes, this is a fact. Even I have been known to start a night out on the Strip this late at night, or early as it may be to some. That is the beauty of living in Vegas, there is something exciting to do at any hour on any night of the week, month, even year.

Las Vegas truly is the city that never sleeps. No one phrases it better than DJ Scotty-boy....

"ITS 4AM IN VEGAS, AND I CAN'T FEEL MY FACE." -DJ SCOTTYBOY

At some point you will eventually get too tired to go on, but don't worry, there is a party going on somewhere in Vegas all the time. In fact, there are so many options it's impossible to go to everything.

Some sleep is necessary, no matter when you squeeze it in. So make sure you allow some room for changes in your itinerary. One night out in Sin City can lead to days, yes days of solid partying, or so I have heard...Lol.

AFTER HOURS NIGHTCLUBS

When you just don't want the night to end, Las Vegas offers many all-night club venues, such as the new Drai's After Hours Nightclub. Formerly located below Bill's Gambling Hall, this ultra modern, hip, all-night dance club provided the option of house music or hip-hop. It may not be the easiest place to get into, especially on the weekend, but once you experience it's one of a kind high-energy dance floor, you will never be the same.

Unfortunately, the original Drai's Nightclub is now closed and has been temporarily moved to Bally's. The new Drai's Dayclub and Nightclub opens in 2014 with a fresh club and a pool. I cannot wait!

Another trendy after-hours location is at the Artisan, Las Vegas' only art hotel. With its dark atmosphere that is very Vampire like, it is the perfect place for those trying to escape the sunrise. The Mood Restaurant located inside the Artisan & unique bar with dancing and music is open around the clock on the weekends. The Artisan also has an exquisite pool area, gardens & a chapel.

LATE NIGHT EDM DANCE VENUES
Drai's
Artisan
Body English
After
Club G
The Black Market Lounge
Club 4427
Club Sesso
Monique Cox
Syn City
Posh
Hush the club
Art Bar
Rise
Club 360 at the Stratosphere

ADULT ENTERTAINMENT

Apart from gambling your night away, there are several other all-night entertainment options, such as Strip clubs to occupy your time.

STRIP CLUB LIST
Spearmint Rhino
Sapphire Gentlemen's Club
Crazy Horse 1 & 2
Crazy Horse 3 (CH3)
Club Paradise
Treasure's
Pussycats
Olympic Gardens
Larry Flint's Hustler Club Can
Can Room Cheetah's
Talk of the Town Babes
Little Darlins
Badda Bing
De Ja Vu
Diamond Cabaret

MALE REVIEWS
Mansion Strip Club
Chippendales
Men of Sapphire
Thunder from Down Under
The Palomino Club
Olympic Gardens

SWINGERS?

Lifestyle Parties are considered sexy adult events, which are very liberal and have an open relationship view of interacting with other couples.

> Fantasy Swingers Club
> Red Rooster
> Green Door
> Show and Tell
> The Drink Sociable Bar
> Power Exchange
> Orchid Lounge

The Red Rooster is a swinger's club on the East side of town near Boulder Highway and Tropicana. You have to get your tickets from the Red Rooster Mini Storage if you would like to partake in the debauchery.

The Green Door is a world famous adult social and swingers club in Las Vegas founded in 1998. Another place I have never been, but have heard tons about it. The sex club earned the title of America's Most Unique Adult Social Club.

ALTERNATIVE BARS

FreeZone
Share
Piranha Nightclub
The Garage
Charlie's
Gipsy Nightclub & Badlands Saloon
Krave

14

TRICKS ARE NOT JUST FOR KIDS

Las Vegas is a very magical and spiritual place. In fact, many predict that Las Vegas will someday be the spiritual mecca of the world.

There are several definitions for the word magic and many who hold the ability to perform illusions and/or bend the rules of reality. In Las Vegas, magic is a common practice and the energy that this city feeds off of is certainly out of the ordinary.

> *Magic can be defined as the art of producing illusions as entertainment by the use of sleight of hand, deceptive devices, etc.*

As the entertainment hub of the galaxy, Las Vegas is extremely fascinating, enchanting and is full of magic. The World's most famous and talented magicians hold residencies in theaters located in many of the cities choice hotels and casinos. Some of these incredible performers include David Copperfield, Penn & Teller, and Criss Angel, to name a few.

These well-known shows can be quite costly; however, there are also hypnotists and smaller shows that are much more affordable located in the not so high-end casinos.

MAGIC SHOWS

CRISS ANGEL BELIEVE
DAVID COPPERFIELD
ILLUSIONS STARRING JAN ROUVEN LAS VEGAS
MAC KING LAS VEGAS MAGIC
MIKE HAMMER COMEDY MAGIC
NATHAN BURTON COMEDY MAGIC
PENN AND TELLER LAS VEGAS
THE MENTALIST IN LAS VEGAS
TOMMY WIND LAS VEGAS

The theater is not the only place to see unforgettable, mind-blowing illusions in Las Vegas. Walking the Strip, you may encounter street magicians that will perform sleight of hand tricks with decks of cards or pull bunnies from a hat.

LOCAL STREET MAGICIANS

RODNEY REYES
CAMERON SHADOW
ADAM FLOWERS PRESTO
MIKE HAMMER STEPHAN
JOHNNY O
WILL ROYA

Rodney Reyes has been transforming ordinary experiences into moments of astounding beauty for over a decade. Now well known as a Celebrity Magician, Rodney Reyes honed his talent in Las Vegas, NV. He built his brand as one of the most exclusive magicians in the United Stages as the resident Magician at Mirage Hotel/Casino and the Resident Magician in Planet Hollywood Casino/Las Vegas.

My personal favorite Street Magician is the infamous Cameron Shadow. He may appear at any moment and leave you completely puzzled from tricks that no matter how closely you watch are simply unexplainable or seemingly impossible.

Be sure to tip, in Vegas a Street Magician is considered a career.

Maybe you would like to take some magic home with you. Try one of these magic shops.

MAGIC STORES

HOUDINI MAGIC SHOP
HOUDINI'S MAGIC SHOP
THE MAGIC SHOP DENNY
AND LEE MAGIC STUDIO
MAGIC COLORS
LITTLE SHOP OF MAGIC

Las Vegas has a vibrant magical energy and has plenty of fortunetellers that can blow your mind with their keen mystic powers. There are plenty of enchanted people willing to read your tarot cards or look into your future.

FORTUNE TELLERS

PSYCHIC FAIRY SPELLS
GREEN EYED WITCH
SUMMERLIN PSYCHIC
READINGS BY LINDA
MONA VAN JOSEPH
YOUR PSYCHIC GUIDE
PSYCHIC KATHERINE
PSYCHIC SPA
BOTANICA ESOTERICA
CATTELL'S STARDATE 2100
GODDESS PSYCHIC SALON
PSYCHIC WORLD
PSYCHIC UNIVERSE
+ HUNDREDS MORE!

Another definition for magic is any extraordinary or mystical influence, charm, or power, etc.

This type of magic is performed by an entirely different realm of magicians, also known as "working girls." The tricks they perform cost far more money and are typically for sexual entertainment. The men who are in search of these promiscuous females are referred to as "tricks."

There are also male escorts that market their services to both women and other men, so don't think it's only the ladies that have a career in this realm. More commonly, these XXX options are available at places like the "Chicken Ranch," as seen on TV.

Girls-for-hire are also advertised on the Strip by the guys that flick their stacks of business cards, which feature the name, number, and photo of available women that do their naughty magic if you have enough cash.

Not all girls in Las Vegas practice this sensual wizardry. Take this as a word of warning girls; you might be labeled as an escort if you are walking alone on the Strip or through a casino in club wear. These assumptions are also true if you are speaking to anyone that's older than your father.

The world we live in is full of assumptions and people say things based off their perception. Even if you are not up to naughty magic, you may still be viewed as a "working girl," due to the friends and activities you are associated with. Being aware of how this all works is guaranteed to assist you in any wanted or unwanted trickery.

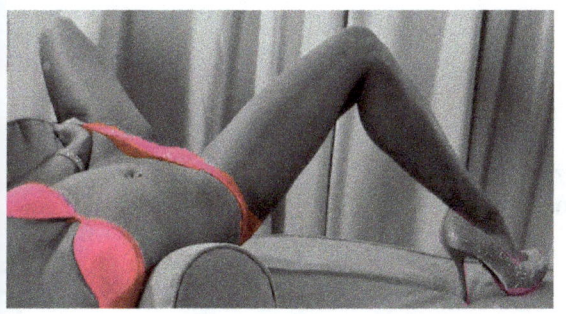

15

LOCAL LIFE

"Locals" have come to accept the crazy unpredictable behavior displayed in Vegas as a way of life.

There is a unique manner business is handled in Las Vegas. Experience is key. Find someone to show you the way, even if you have studied up. The best idea is to find a VIP host or local that is willing to guide you and show you the ropes.

For those of you reading this that have friends in Vegas, there are a few things you should know. The journey back to where ever "home" is for you is a far different from that of a local.

You see... locals have made this a lifestyle. This means when you get home and things get back to "normal" for you, we "locals" will still be doing the same thing...Day after day... Night after night....

Please do not take offense if you come to visit a local and you find them hungover or unwilling to participate in "tourist activities."

Keeping up with daily responsibilities when living on a permanent vacation, in the most exciting city on the planet, requires more energy than some sports.

A Las Vegas local is expected to retain an enormous amount of information. It is almost as if all residents are trained to know the basic facts of Las Vegas with the ability to give directions within a moment's notice.

Finding a balance between spending time with friends that are visiting and your local affiliates may seem tedious and exhausting, but that balance is vital to achieve success here.

There are also some locals that it seems almost everyone who has gone out to a nightclub/after hours in Vegas knows. A perfect example is one of my best friends, Neldy.

THE MUSIC SCENE

The widespread expansion on the West Coast of electronic music is comparable to a submissive DJ takeover. In the local Las Vegas music scene thrives on the arrival of celebrities and world renown DJs such as; David Guetta, Benny Benassi, Tiesto, Erick Morillo, Deadmau5, Afrojack, Steve Aoki, Donald Glaude, Calvin Harris, Skrillex & Kaskade.

For those of you asking yourself, "Who?" Have no fear, because one trip to Las Vegas and it will be very difficult to miss the presence of the world's best DJ performers.

These trendsetting musicians are using Las Vegas to establish their role as a DJ in a way that has never been attempted, forever changing our local culture as well as electronic music around the world.

Now I am not saying electronic music is all you will hear in Las Vegas nightclubs. Of course mainstream top 40 radio and hip-hop will always have a place in what is heard, wherever you go in the world. After all, meeting Snoop Dogg (Snoop Lion) at the Playboy Mansion is part of the reason I ended up moving to Sin City.

With these amazing entertainers performing at different times 24 hours a day, 7 days a week, those people living in Las Vegas are faced with another challenge... SLEEP. I am extremely disciplined and yet still I am faced with a common local difficulty: there are simply not enough hours in a day to attend all the options available in Vegas.

You never know what you will wake up to in Vegas, considering this is one place that anything could happen.

"Social norms" are a difficult topic to discern, due to the social complexity of the city.

"Weird" is viewed as a good thing to most people here, in fact the weirder the better.

Industry jobs have a different definition and require an entirely separate skill set than that of any other city. The first step to becoming a host is get a business card and learn your way around.

"Ladies, if you are sleeping with a VIP host, don't be surprised if you find out the other 20 girls on his guest list are too." –Chella

RELATIONSHIPS IN VEGAS

If you are looking for the low down on relationships in Sin City, to put it very plainly...it's complicated. Lol. In any relationship it is difficult to establish trust and resist temptation, but it is nearly impossible in Vegas. Especially when you consider that your special someone could succumb to his or her worst addictions and change into someone completely different overnight. Sin City was built to cater to addicts. If you live in Vegas, you will definitely come across someone gambling or selling drugs/ sex. Some can ignore it, but some fall victim to their inner desires.

One thing is for sure, if you are going to attempt dating a local...be willing to forgive. The opportunities and scenarios created here are hard to resist. Honesty is a must, but at the same time, if you explained every small detail things could easily be misconstrued.

When complications arise, it is essential that you can talk about issues and come to an understanding. If you happen to experience an argument or breakup in Sin City, my best advice is "Get over it, or get under it." The only problem with this is the fact that Vegas is such a big small town that status changes and relationship drama is highly viral, meaning word can travel fast.

Don't limit yourself by only dating another local. There are millions of people that are consistently traveling through the never ending revolving door of excitement.

Now I am not saying that it's impossible to find the love of your life here, I am just giving you a reality check that coming to Sin City to find the man or woman of your dreams may not be the best idea. This spontaneous city is definitely designed for those that are single over families and those looking for love.

However, there are more wedding chapels here than anywhere else in the country. Las Vegas has celebrated love through bachelor/bachelorette parties to weddings to honeymoons to anniversaries for many more years than I have even been alive, so this is something you may have to discover on your own.

In order to be loved, you must love yourself. When trying to meet someone new, if you want be treated with respect, you must demand it and carry yourself with confidence.
Lead by example and don't fall victim to peer pressure, destroying your values and morals for someone that doesn't need to be in your life anyway.

16

CHECKING OUT

Knowing when it is time to count your chips and return to reality...even if you live here.

DEPARTING SIN CITY IS TYPICALLY A STRUGGLE, TO SAY THE LEAST. SOME VISITORS BEGIN PLANNING THEIR NEXT TRIP BACK TO LAS VEGAS BEFORE THEY EVEN LEAVE.

OTHERS REFUSE TO LEAVE.

Not even the bellman can remove someone who has firmly decided this city is where they belong. That's basically much what happened to me...my 3 day trips became 3 week extended stays, too many times for me to continue fighting against making the move west from Ohio any longer.

It makes sense that a place as incredible as Vegas would be difficult to pull yourself away from. Of course after 5 days on a streak of living like a local, it may seem like a great idea to round it up to a week and make it 7 days instead.

For those that live life on the lavish side, being spoiled and waited on hand and foot with 5 star VIP treatment is definitely hard to resist. Well, for most people that is not

the case, but it can be if you have the right resources and know the right people.

It's common that the last thing on your mind is going home, but if you have responsibilities the trip has to end at some point. Although some visitors stay longer than expected because they don't want to leave, there are also people that stay because they simply can't leave. Some due to lack of funds, for others, it's the result of excessive partying and extreme hangovers.

> Maybe you have heard the expression, "You don't have to go home, but you can't stay here."

Even those that live here have problems leaving the electric glow of the neon strip. For example, my friend Katie once missed four flights when departing LAS on a group vacation for our friend's birthday. Four flights? Really? Lol... Only in Vegas.

Be sure to check the club photo sites for any pictures you may or may not remember taking. If you do have your picture taken by the local 702 paparazzi, ask for a business card from them (more clues from any times that may appear a bit blurry).

Do your best to leave with a good attitude and not be a sore loser. Do things because you enjoy them and not because you simply desire the honor of winning. You can only blame yourself if you do not enjoy your time in Vegas.

When it comes to borrowing and accepting money, my lawyer and one of my best friend's Steve has some advice for you as well.

"Always take the money when it's offered to you and don't write a check with your mouth that you can't cash with your ass." -Steve Aaronoff

EVEN IF YOU LEAVE WITH HALF OF WHAT YOU STARTED CONSIDER YOURSELF A WINNER.

Not everyone succeeds at winning the jackpot. Although some people have hit big, do not expect that once you have lost the majority of your cash that you are going to magically win your money back.

If you do happen to lose all of your money or get yourself into a situation that leaves you questioning your morals, take a deep breath and just know that...

EVERYTHING IS GOING TO BE OK! OR AS NANA WOULD SAY, "WHAT'S MEANT TO BE WILL BE."

You can't win them all, so cut yourself some slack. This city was not created for everyone to win every time. Remember that if you do have to leave, you can always come back.

17

PLUS TIP

Make your tip memorable!

When leaving a tip at a bar for instance, you should not wait until right before you walk away to toss out a few ones your first trip to the bar.

This is definitely a city where enough money can make almost anything a possibility. For those of you with a limited budget, it is important to spend wisely.

You may be from somewhere in which tipping is optional; however, in Las Vegas tipping is a crucial part of day-to-day life here.

My best advice to those of you going to a club that choose not to get bottle service is to pick one specific bartender to get your drinks from for the night and start out with a larger tip. Depending on the number of drinks being ordered, around $20 should work out pretty well. The next time only tip $5-15, roughly $2-4 per drink is standard in a club.

When tipping the bartender a general rule of tipping $1-2 per drink is average. If it is a high-end establishment you will have to use your own judgement.

For Bottle Service, expect to tip 15-25% of the total, but look at your bill carefully as gratuity is included at some locations.

Casino Cocktail servers can also be tipped with chips as well as cash. Standard tipping is $1-5 per drink depending on what you order, what you are playing, and what casino you are in, and what your budget is.

The Dealer should be tipped $1 per winning hand or $5-20 per hour depending on how much the table is per hand and your winnings. For large winnings, it is customary to tip the dealer by chip.

When I gamble, I will bet $1 on the line ahead of my marker so that if I win, the dealer wins the $1 bet (plus with a chip for my hand that's obviously larger than $1).

Restaurant servers should be tipped 15-25%. In some restaurants gratuity will automatically be added to your bill.

Buffet servers should be given $1 per person or per drink.

Room Service should be tipped 15-20%.

Concierge are usually expecting at least $5 per task.

The Front Desk clerk may even be able to give you a "complimentary upgrade" when slipped a $20 tip.

Bell Service should be tipped $2-3 per bag.

Pool Attendants should be given $1-2 per person.

Taxis are usually expecting at least a 10% tip. Limos more like 15-20%.

Valet should be tipped $2-10 for dropping off your car, and $3-10 at pickup.

Hosts should be tipped $10-30 per person for actions such as being placed on the guest list, or other means of free entry.

The Door Host should be tipped $20 or more per person for skipping the line.

Bathroom attendants should be tipped $1 per visit, $2-5 if you use their supplies.

Tour Guides should be given a minimum of $1 per person, depending on the length of the tour, personality and the overall experience

Entertainers should always be tipped when doing personal entertainment. Some examples would be Super Hero and Celebrity look-a-likes (his can be as low as $2 per picture), street musicians, etc. Performers in shows have their performance fees paid by the theater or "house."

Magicians doing a special performance at your table should be tipped $10-20+ up to $100+ depending on the trick and the size of your group.

Strippers should be handled at your own discretion.

BE SURE TO THANK EVERYONE. TIPPING IS IMPORTANT. MAKE YOUR TIP MEMORABLE.

For all of you Las Vegas Locals, when you are joining a comped table at one of the city's legendary nightclubs, it is polite to offer to throw in for the bottle. You are still required to tip on comped bottles. $20 is usually a fair amount to pay per person.

Ladies if you get the invitation to one of the free girl's dinners, be on time and prepared to tip for your comped dinner ($20 per girl is customary). This typically includes your dinner, drinks and club entry. The $20 is more than fair.

18

702 TRIVIA

Time to see what you know about the most exciting city in the world. For the most part the majority of visitors and residents focus their attention on the now, rather than the history of Las Vegas, but these are some cool facts everyone should know.

FACTS FOR FOREIGN VISITORS

If visiting from a foreign country outside of North America, you may require an electrical adapter for your electronics. Las Vegas uses 110 to 120 volts AC (60 cycles) electrical outlets and accept the standard North American plug with two flat parallel pins.

The Las Vegas telephone area code is 702. For any emergency requiring police or medical assistance call 911 (toll-free).

The sales tax in Las Vegas is an 8.1% sales tax on purchases, however there is a 12% tax on hotel rooms. There is a 13% tax on hotel rooms located near the Fremont Street Experience in Downtown Las Vegas.

HISTORY

Discovered in 1829 by Spanish explorers, Las Vegas was known at that time as "The Meadows." Established as a watering place for travelers headed to California, the Mormons were attracted to the area's artesian water and settled the land in 1855. 2 years later the Mormons abandoned the site, and the US Army established Ft. Baker in what was considered property of Arizona in 1864. In 1867, the land was detached from Arizona and joined with the Nevada territory.

LOCATED IN CLARK COUNTY, LAS VEGAS IS THE 31ST MOST POPULATED CITY IN THE UNITED STATES AND HOME OF THE MOST FAMOUS STREET IN THE UNIVERSE, LAS VEGAS BLVD (LVB), AKA "THE STRIP." THIS

ICONIC ROADWAY IS 4.2 MILES OF EXTREME ENTERTAINMENT. THE 2ND FAMOUS STREET WITHIN THE CITY WOULD BE FREMONT STREET.

The "Vegas Valley" includes unincorporated communities such as Paradise, Winchester, and Enterprise.

Pahrump, Laughlin, Mesquite, Boulder City and Mt. Charleston are cities within close proximity to Vegas. Interstate I-15 is the main transit for visitors driving to and from Las Vegas. The I-215 is the outer belt that surrounds the Strip.

HAUNTED VEGAS

Haunted Vegas? My opinion is yes, even my house is haunted. Lol.

The Flamingo is said to be the most haunted place in Las Vegas, as it was home to one of the biggest mobsters to ever walk the Strip.

Legend has it that Bugsy Siegel lived in the best suite in the hotel until he was murdered by fellow mobsters and buried in the rose garden at the Flamingo. Bugsy's ghost is still known to haunt the casino and his apparition can be visible late at night in the rose garden.

Liberace is another spirit that is yet to reach his next/final destination. The Liberace museum and restaurant is the location for this paranormal activity.

VEGAS NOW

Each year millions of tourists come to Vegas. That is over 39,727,022 visitors who travel to Sin City according to the LVCVA.

THE NUMBER OF RESIDENTS THAT LIVE FULL TIME IN LAS VEGAS IS A POPULATION OF 583,756. THAT IS 294,100 MEN AND 289,656 WOMEN THAT ARE BRAVE/CRAZY/WEIRD ENOUGH TO CONSIDER LAS VEGAS HOME.

For the past 18 years, Las Vegas has led the United States as the best location for conventions. Last year Las Vegas held 21,615 conventions held in Sin City.

Some of the biggest and most sought after conventions to attend are Super Zoo (pet convention), Magic (fashion), CES (computers) and SEMA (Specialty Equipment Marketing Association).

EDC alone brings in over 300,000 partiers to dance in the desert for the ritual electronic music festival. These dance music followers spend a whopping $278 million in Clark County during the event, spending their money on much more than just glow sticks.

The local College in Vegas is University of Nevada, Las Vegas (UNLV). The sport's team for UNLV is the Runnin Rebels. I can imagine it would be tough to resist all of the distractions from the Strip only 1.5 miles away, however with determination it can be done. My business partner, Rick Lofton, is a UNLV graduate.

First Friday is an event in downtown Vegas that takes place the first Friday of every month. This day celebrates art, music, food and entertainment with food trucks, Kid-Zone., GreenZone and live bands. Every month the event runs from 5pm-12am.

The Bellagio is not only the site of a beautiful greenhouse with seasonal decor that is exceptionally designed, but it also has a garden with a horticulture facility on the roof. Restaurants within the casino actually use the tomatoes grown on the roof in their food!

THE HOOVER DAM IS AN ARCH-GRAVITY DAM LOCATED IN THE BLACK CANYON OF THE COLORADO RIVER.

The Hoover dam was originally constructed in 1931 & 1936 during the Great Depression. It was highly advanced for its time and is a hydroelectric power plant.

Las Vegas is home to many Native Americans, primarily the Mohave Indians. I had the honor of meeting some of their chiefs at the dedication of the Hoover Dam bypass.

The completion of the bypass was significant due to the ability for the first time in history for transporting goods to and from Nevada and Arizona.

19

FAQ

Why is my skin so dry?
Everything is dry here. Lotion and water are a no brainer.

Does Las Vegas have any hot springs?
Yes, Nevada has more than 350 natural hot springs! That is far more than any other state.

Is there more than 1 airport?

Yes, the main airport is McCarren Airport, which has 2 terminals. There are actually more than 30 airports in Las Vegas including: Henderson Municipal Airport, North Las Vegas Airport, Nellis and the Franien Airport off of Sunset Rd.

Is Area 51 in Vegas?

Area 51 / S4 information including getting your very own alien license for only $4.95 can be found at http://www.insidervlv.com/area51/info.html

Are there really people living in the sewers?

I have never been down there, but it does make sense. In an article in one of the local papers, I read there are over 300 miles of sewer tunnels that are home to thousands of people beneath the streets of Las Vegas. My heart goes out to those poor souls every time it begins to rain heavily. The dry desert ground does not absorb water easily and the slightest accumulation of rain causes severe flooding, which would wash away the makeshift homes these subsurface dwellers have created.

Is there a curfew for those under 18?

Yes. Sorry kids. All kids under 18 should be accompanied by an adult. If you are under the age of 18, you must be off of the Strip by 10pm! Even on the weekends. :(

How easy is it to get married in Vegas?

For legal requirements and information on getting married in Clark County, please visit Clark County Marriage License Bureau.

Why does everyone seem to have the same job?

There is probably a convention. Most every industry in the world holds an annual convention in Vegas. This is not simply because every market feels they need a reason to come and party for a few days a year, more so it is because the things that happen in this magical city grasp the attention of the entire world.

Why won't any taxis pick up on the Strip?

Taxis cannot pick you up on the Strip, only from a casino valet.

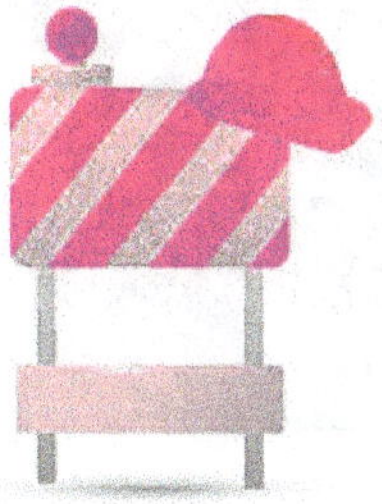

Why is there so much construction?

Las Vegas is constantly changing and expanding, unfortunately the roadwork is inevitable.

Is there a Monorail?

Yes, it runs from Sahara to MGM and you can view the schedule at www.lvmonorail.com A single ride is $5 and a one-day pass is $12.

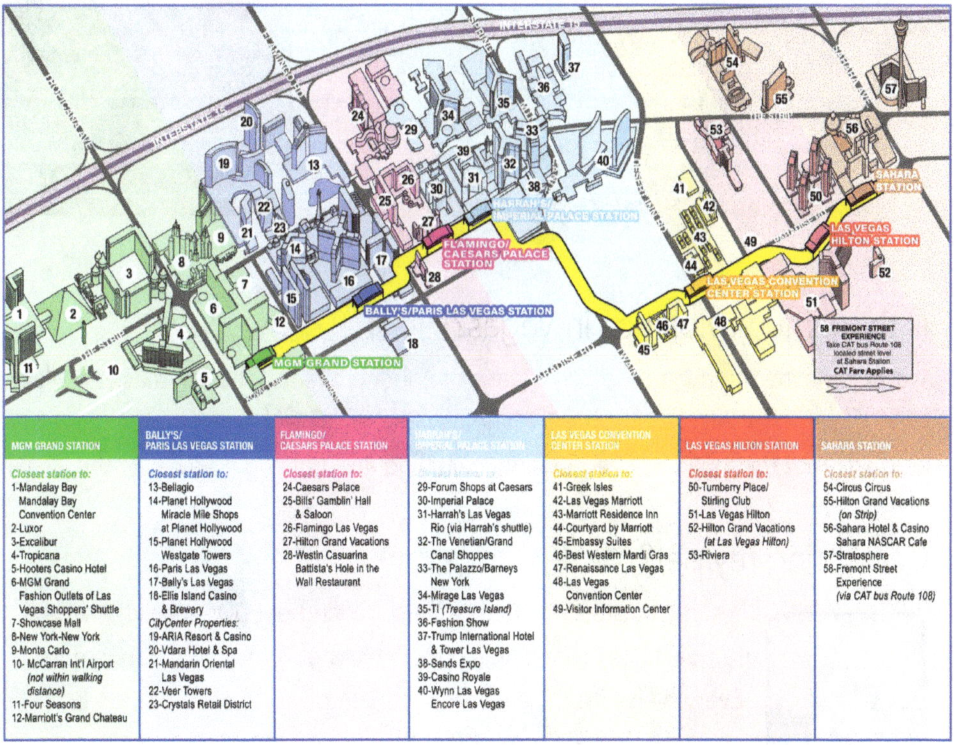

MGM GRAND STATION	BALLY'S/ PARIS LAS VEGAS STATION	FLAMINGO/ CAESARS PALACE STATION	HARRAH'S/ IMPERIAL PALACE STATION	LAS VEGAS CONVENTION CENTER STATION	LAS VEGAS HILTON STATION	SAHARA STATION
Closest station to: 1-Mandalay Bay Mandalay Bay Convention Center 2-Luxor 3-Excalibur 4-Tropicana 5-Hooters Casino Hotel 6-MGM Grand Fashion Outlets of Las Vegas Shoppers' Shuttle 7-Showcase Mall 8-New York-New York 9-Monte Carlo 10- McCarran Int'l Airport *(not within walking distance)* 11-Four Seasons 12-Marriott's Grand Chateau	*Closest station to:* 13-Bellagio 14-Planet Hollywood Miracle Mile Shops at Planet Hollywood 15-Planet Hollywood Westgate Towers 16-Paris Las Vegas 17-Bally's Las Vegas 18-Ellis Island Casino & Brewery *CityCenter Properties:* 19-ARIA Resort & Casino 20-Vdara Hotel & Spa 21-Mandarin Oriental Las Vegas 22-Veer Towers 23-Crystals Retail District	*Closest station to:* 24-Caesars Palace 25-Bills' Gamblin' Hall & Saloon 26-Flamingo Las Vegas 27-Hilton Grand Vacations 28-Westin Casuarina Battista's Hole in the Wall Restaurant	*Closest station to:* 29-Forum Shops at Caesars 30-Imperial Palace 31-Harrah's Las Vegas Rio (via Harrah's shuttle) 32-The Venetian/Grand Canal Shoppes 33-The Palazzo/Barneys New York 34-Mirage Las Vegas 35-TI *(Treasure Island)* 36-Fashion Show 37-Trump International Hotel & Tower Las Vegas 38-Sands Expo 39-Casino Royale 40-Wynn Las Vegas Encore Las Vegas	*Closest station to:* 41-Greek Isles 42-Las Vegas Marriott 43-Marriott Residence Inn 44-Courtyard by Marriott 45-Embassy Suites 46-Best Western Mardi Gras 47-Renaissance Las Vegas 48-Las Vegas Convention Center 49-Visitor Information Center	*Closest station to:* 50-Turnberry Place/ Stirling Club 51-Las Vegas Hilton 52-Hilton Grand Vacations *(at Las Vegas Hilton)* 53-Riviera	*Closest station to:* 54-Circus Circus 55-Hilton Grand Vacations *(on Strip)* 56-Sahara Hotel & Casino Sahara NASCAR Cafe 57-Stratosphere 58-Fremont Street Experience *(via CAT bus Route 108)*

Do many celebrities live in Vegas?
Absolutely. There are a countless number of entertainers, athletes, and other social icons that consider themselves a citizen of Sin City, but only some acquire the official Nevada ID card. Coolio has his VIP Vegas ID. lol.

Is it expensive to live in Las Vegas?
Well, that all depends on your budget. I have found it to be reasonable when it comes to rent, gas and general expenses. It is definitely more affordable than living in Los Angeles.

Do I really live in "Laser World?"
Well, yes. My Las Vegas Bachelorette Pad has become known as "Laser World." My 2 story residence is filled with gadgets and an energy that inspires me with creative ideas for PetBlaster.

This location is known for "Breakfast @Tiffani's."

Is there much violence in Vegas?
Yes, but mostly to drive tourism by means of fighting events. The Thomas and Mack, MGM, Rio, Orleans, Hard Rock and Mandalay Bay, along with several other casinos, hold some of the most watched boxing, wrestling and fighting matches in the world.

Can I bring my pet?

Yes, my business specializes in supplying pet owners with answers to questions just like this one. PetBlaster is "Your One Source for Everything Pets™" and connects pet owners to the people & products they are looking for. Please sign up for a free profile at www.PetBlaster.com.

Why does everyone always flash a claw in my photos?

Rawr! The Claw! Raising a claw is just something fun we do in our pictures be-claws we can.

Jeff Davis is officially the King of Claws.

Is there an age that is too old to go to Vegas?

Of course not! I even took my parents and Nana to Tao! They even met Carrot Top. Lol. Age is simply a number. You are only as old as you allow yourself to be.

Nana was also featured in her local Newspaper, the Daily Jeffersonian for her first visit to Sin City. She may not be the next show girl, but she sure does love the slot machines.

Cambridge resident Betty Zvolensky, l, traveled to Las Vegas to visit granddaughter Tiffani Neilson. While there, they stopped by famous Fremont Street to have their photo taken with a showgirl holding up a copy of *The Daily & Sunday Jeffersonian*. Also on the trip were Michael and Lisa Neilson.

Hello, Jeffland!

These are the final two submissions for the 2010 edition of "Hello, Jeffland!"

This newspaper's annual vacation photograph feature was again well received with more than 230 photos submitted.

Look for a special report from "Hello, Jeffland!" coordinator and newsroom staffer Dan Davis, coming soon.

Thanks to all readers who submitted photographs.

20

ARE YOU A SIN CITY SURVIVOR?

IN ORDER TO KNOW WHO YOU TRULY ARE, YOU MUST TEST YOUR BOUNDARIES.

WHAT ARE YOU WILLING TO GAMBLE OR SETTLE FOR? HOW DOES YOUR EGO MAINTAIN WHEN ALL ODDS ARE AGAINST YOU? DO YOU HAVE WHAT IT TAKES TO FAKE IT TILL YOU MAKE IT, OR AT LEAST UNTIL YOU HAVE THE

FUNDING TO PARTY LIKE A PRO? IS IT ABOUT WINNING AT THE CASINO OR ABOUT WINNING IN LIFE? HOW MUCH ARE YOU WILLING TO RISK TO MAKE YOUR DREAMS INTO REALITIES? AT WHAT POINT DO YOU WALK AWAY & ACCEPT THAT YOU DO NOT HAVE WHAT IT TAKES TO SURVIVE IN SIN CITY? WHAT IS YOUR GOAL? WHAT WILL IT TAKE FOR YOU TO HIT THE MARK & CONSIDER YOURSELF A WINNER?

Life is full of challenges no matter where you live and what your lifestyle is. Without the bad times, we would not be able to appreciate the good things.

For any of you "Vegas Virgins" out there, why are you still stalling? Start saving and strategizing. If you want something bad enough, nothing can stand in your way.

No one and no place is ever going to be perfect. There is no "perfect" vacation. It's about making the most of what you have. Enjoy the journey as much as your destination.

Focus on what you want and in time your problems will become your solutions. It is through our mistakes that we are able to grow as a person. If you are facing an issue, ask yourself if it even worth your time & energy to be upset about. Life is too short to waste on things that will not make your soul smile in eternity.

Whether you are simply visiting or reside in Sin City, it does not take a zombie apocalypse to test your survival skills. Las Vegas has a way of confronting your fears & flaws, tempting you in every way imaginable. They do call it Sin City for a reason.
My mind, body and soul have endured 5 years in this 702 circus. My character, values, patience, and tolerance have been thoroughly tested and then some.

If you're considering moving to Las Vegas, I am proof it is possible to survive in Sin City. The demanding & luxurious life of a VIP Las Vegas Local is like living in a movie filled with plenty of action, comedy and drama. Balance is essential; along with thick skin that can shake off negativity and petty confrontations.

THE BOTTOM LINE IS IN ORDER TO SURVIVE IN LAS VEGAS, YOU HAVE TO ... SUCK IT UP OR GET SUCKED UP. LAS VEGAS CAN EAT YOU ALIVE! IF YOU ARE NOT WILLING TO STRUGGLE, FALL DOWN, LOSE AND PICK YOURSELF BACK UP AGAIN WITH CONFIDENCE, DON'T EXPECT YOU HAVE WHAT IT TAKES TO SWIM WITH THE DESERT SHARKS.

As much as the sun's powerful rays can warm your soul, the dry desolate desert can fade its vibrancy. You only have one chance and one life to do everything you ever wanted, so plan ahead & make the most of it.

Sin City makes ALMOST anything available for the right price, but money can't buy happiness. Happiness is a choice that you are forced to take action on daily. Be grateful, be realistic, be positive, be whoever and whatever it is that you want to be.

Personally, I feel that if you can look yourself in the mirror every day and continue to love the person you see with a smile... you have succeeded. This city has the power to transform people, for the good or the bad.

I have seen Vegas chew people up and spit them out faster than their planned vacation would allow. I have also witnessed this adult fantasy world lift people up to their highest level of self.

WOULD YOU CONSIDER YOURSELF A SIN CITY SURVIVOR?

IF NOT, IT'S NEVER TOO LATE, SO START BOOKING YOUR NEXT TRIP!

Solutions for all your how-to-702 travel needs are available at www.SinCitySurvivalGuide.com.

Don't forget to tell your friends.
See you in Sin City!

21

GLOSSARY

5 Points; (noun) Intersection of Charleston, Boulder, Fremont, Eastern & 25th streets.
86ed; (verb) Permanently banned or kicked out.
Area 51; (noun) Fact or fictional place known to be the intergalactic alien airport.
Ball; (noun) When an individual or group has a great time.(verb) Spend money.
Baller; (noun) To be or act as a someone who likes to flaunt or show that he or she has money or possessions
Bang; (verb) An action, in slang it means to have sex or to do work, "bang it out."

Beast; (noun) Males - Muscular, Aggressive, Steroid Freaks.
Booty Call; (noun) This is that call that is for the sole purpose of sexual intercourse. Usually made between the hours of 2am-12pm ,but in Vegas everything is 24 hours.
Bottle Service; (noun) A designated area for purchase of a bottle and rental of premiere nightclub real estate.
Boxman; (noun) The craps table dealer who sits over the drop box and supervises the bets and payoffs.
Break Bread; (verb) To spend cash or make things right by forking over money.
Bunk; (adj) No good, fake
Busted; (adj) Locked in Jail.
Carson; (place) How northern Nevadans say Carson City.
Coupons; (noun) Redeemable for nearly everything from a free meal to a free pull on a slot machine. (Ask the hotel whether it has a coupon book.)
Cut; (verb) Deleted or kicked out of a relationship, friendship or group.
Dark; (adj) No show; as in Dark Sundays means no shows on Sunday.
Drop box; (noun) A locked box located on live gambling tables where dealers deposit paper money.
Escort; (noun) A male or female who is paid for their time to hang out and or exchange sexual activities.
Eye in the sky; (noun) A one-way mirror surveillance in the casino area. Be sure to smile! Mirrors or dark glass that circles casino ceilings conceals people who are assigned to watch the casino action to prevent cheating by players or dealers. There are also cameras behind the decorative looking glass.
Faded; (adj) Wasted or intoxicated.
Frenemy; (noun) A person that pretends to be your friend but is really your enemy.
Groupie; (noun) Males or females that feel cooler by following a popular individual of famous star.
Hater; (noun) Someone who is jealous and hates on another human being.
Health Card: (noun) A health card is required for most employees, especially those working as a food or beverage handler.
Hella; (adj) Originally created in the San Francisco Bay Area as a synonym for very.
High roller; (noun) A customer with the reputation of wagering large sums of money in the casino.
Hit me; (phrase) A phrase used by blackjack players who want another card from the dealer. Usually used accompanying a hand signal.

Host; (noun) An individual that gets clientele anything they desire. Usually sets a client up with bottle service at the club.

In red; (adj) A comped customer's name usually appears "in red" on a maitre d's reservation chart.

Industry Night; (noun) A dedicated night to all the people who work in the club or service industry (Usually a great night to network and make connections with locals).

Industry; (noun) A term used to reference people employed in the night life industry.

Jaded; (adj) The state or being worn out by the Las Vegas Lifestyle.

Limit; (noun) The least or maximum bet accepted at a gambling table.

Local; (noun) A person or thing of residence in Las Vegas (for reference while in Sin City).

Marker; (noun) An IOU owed the casino by a gambler allowed by the hotel to play on credit.

Meh; (adj) Used to describe a person, place, thing as pretty much anything you don't really want to say or used as a feeling or mood that is very blah. It can also be something that doesn't matter.

Negative Nancy; (noun) Someone that is being negative. AKA Debbie Downer.

On Deck; (adj) In Hand, has access to a certain product.

On Fire; (adj) On a roll, too hot to stop.

PetBlaster; (noun) The Ultimate Pet Social Network and "Your One Source for Everything Pets.™" www.PetBlaster.com

Pit boss; (noun) A casino boss who oversees numerous table dealers.

Scaria 51; (noun) This is an area near Primm, NV that is said to be extremely haunted. Buffalo Bills is home to many ghost sightings.

Selfie: (noun) An image someone takes of themselves, most commonly used for posting on social media.

Sheriff's Card; (noun) A work card that must be obtained by the State of Nevada before beginning work in the gaming or liquor industry.

Shoe; (noun) A container from which several decks of cards are dealt on the Baccarat and blackjack tables which prevents the dealer from holding cards.

Shooter; (noun) A gambler who is rolling the dice on a craps table.

Smash N Bounce; (noun) A one night stand.

Spoon; (noun) One device used by slot machine cheaters.

Stalker; (noun) A male or female that just simply won't leave you alone.

Stickman; (noun) The dealer who moves the dice around on a craps table with a hook shaped stick.

Strapped; (adj) Carrying a weapon or wearing a condom.

Strip/ The Strip; (noun) Las Vegas Blvd.

Swingers; (noun) A couple seeking sex playmate.

TAM Card; (noun) TAM cards are required for servers, sellers and security cards. This "Drink Card" signifies the completion of Alcohol Awareness Training.

Tip; (verb) Same as a toke or gratuity.

Trop; (noun) Short for Tropicana hotel and casino.

Vegas Prom; (noun) Vegas Prom is an annual event thrown by Botown Productions that is pretty much a popularity contest amongst locals in the "industry." Even getting nominated for the court is considered an honor.

Walk of Shame; (noun) Takes place when the sun rises. When an individual wears the same clothes from the night before after making out with a complete stranger.

Wasted; (adj) Drunk with blurred vision. One should not drive wasted in Las Vegas. What What; (exclamation) The universal double-what signifies what being questioned on many levels, often used used as an optimistic exclamation; such as: yay! or Woohoo!

Working Girl; (noun) Escort, Pay to Play.

Zen; (noun) The feeling of a properly executed Vegas activity or vacation.